MODERN AND CONTEMPORARY SWISS POETRY: AN ANTHOLOGY

OTHER WORKS IN THE DALKEY ARCHIVE PRESS'S
SWISS LITERATURE SERIES

Isle of the Dead
Gerhard Meier

Walaschek's Dream
Giovanni Orelli

Why the Child Is Cooking in the Polenta
Aglaja Veteranyi

With the Animals
Noëlle Revaz

The Shadow of Memory
Bernard Comment

MODERN AND CONTEMPORARY SWISS POETRY: AN ANTHOLOGY

EDITED AND WITH AN INTRODUCTION BY LUZIUS KELLER

TRANSLATED BY

SIMON KNIGHT
REINHARD MAYER
DONAL MCLAUGHLIN
BURTON PIKE
JAMIE RICHARDS
JOHN TAYLOR
AND
LAUREN K. WOLFE

Library of Congress Cataloging-in-Publication Data

Modern and contemporary Swiss poetry : an anthology / edited and with an
introduction by Luzius Keller ; translated by Simon Knight . . . [et al.].
    p. cm.
A selection of the work of Switzerland's greatest poets of the twentieth century
and their contemporary counterparts, translated from the country's major lan-
guages -- French, Italian, Rhaeto-Romanic, and German.
    ISBN 978-1-56478-788-0 (cloth : alk. paper)
    1. Swiss poetry--20th century--Translations into English. 2. Swiss poetry--
21st century--Translations into English. I. Knight, Simon.
    PN849.S92M63 2012
    808.81'99494--dc23
                                    2012030549

Please see Rights and Permissions on page 371 for individual credits.

This anthology has been generously supported by the Max Geilinger-Stiftung
in celebration of its 50th Anniversary. The Foundation was established in 1962
in Zurich, Switzerland, to promote the literary and cultural relations between
Switzerland and the English-speaking world.

The publication of this work was supported by a grant from Pro Helvetia, Swiss
Arts Council.

Partially funded by a grant from the Illinois Arts Council, a state agency.

Grateful acknowledgment is also made for the input and support of Translation
House Looren.

Max Geilinger-Stiftung   swiss arts council
                                   prohelvetia   ARTS

Cover: design and composition by Mikhail Iliatov
Printed on permanent/durable acid-free paper and bound in the United States
of America
www.dalkeyarchive.com

TABLE OF CONTENTS

INTRODUCTION | XV

I
FRENCH

II
ITALIAN

INTRODUCTION

Gränzä	Borders
Ich bi ganz verpiiluts	I'm all banged up
vam Aaschlaa a nu eigenu Gränzä	from knocking against my own borders
aber	yet
hintemaal	now and again
ggraatut mr der Schprung	I manage
druber	to leap them

BERNADETTE LERJEN-SARBACH

Switzerland is no borderland, but it is a land of borders: national borders, cantonal borders, community borders, linguistic borders—some barely noticeable, others very real impediments to the communal life of the regions and their inhabitants. Borders mark its poets as well. Certainly, Fabio Pusterla has translated Philippe Jaccottet and Corinna Bille; Giorgio Orelli, Andri Peer; Andri Peer, Maurice Chappaz; José-Flore Tappy, Erika Burkart; Donata Berra, Klaus Merz . . . Certainly, Elisabeth Meylan and Niklaus Meienberg listen to Blaise Cendrars; Andri Peer to Albin Zollinger; Frédéric Wandelère and Vanni Bianconi to everything that goes on around them . . . Certainly, the blackbird sings (and dies) in Gerhard Meier as well as in Giorgio Orelli, and both Fabio Pusterla and Leta Semadeni give voice to the lament of cattle led to slaughter. And yet, despite all cultural and political efforts, collective appearances in anthologies and other publications, literature conferences, readings, or round-table discussions—one still cannot speak of a specifically Swiss lyric poetry. This is, however, our good fortune, it must be said—for when a poet is handed a yardstick, he runs the risk of losing his own measure, his own voice.

This measuring-out of one's own space and its borders is addressed, for example, in the poems of Bernadette Lerjen-Sarbach, written in the dialect of the Upper Valais, a language that for not a few Swiss German ears lies, indeed, beyond the frontier of the comprehensible. Lyricism, however, knows no boundaries. It opens itself to every ear. This is confirmed by the musical setting of "Gränzä" ("Borders") by the Swiss composer Heinz Holliger, which itself explores the border areas between poetry and music, language and sound, noise and stillness. Ludwig Hohl too has declared border regions to be the proper locus of art and literature. In *Von den hereinbrechenden Rändern* (From the Collapsing Margins, published posthumously in 1986) he speaks of "marginal districts" ("Randbezirken"), the "unraveling places of secondary effects" ("zerfasernden Orten der Nebenerscheinungen"), where new ideas are ripe for discovery and able to develop.

Some of the poets brought together in this volume move—socially as well as physically—in just such marginal districts: Edmond-Henri Crisinel, Robert Walser, Regina Ullmann, Adelheid Duvanel, and Alexander Xaver Gwerder, to name only a few . . . And even the boundaries of decorum may be trespassed by literature. Thus Giovanni Orelli lets his hero relieve himself by the front door of a tavern, and Dumenic Andry fills twenty-one lines with, by and large, the most indelicate expletives. And yet, Orelli's vernacular burlesque and Andry's blue streak quite clearly have more substance than many a sonnet from the south of Switzerland composed in sterling Italian, or many a small, finely crafted poem from the Grisons. In Kurt Marti's "hommage à rabelais," vulgar words are even seen to become a fountain in the desert of the loveliest words.

This anthology begins with the poets of Francophone Switzerland—*la Suisse romande*—and with one poet in particular, who initially declined what Paul Nizon termed a "discourse in narrowness," turning his back on his homeland in his youth. Blaise Cendrars, born Frédéric-Louis Sauser, passes beyond not only the borders of his country, but also the boundaries of classical meter. Moscow, St. Petersburg, Paris, and New York were the first stations of his turbulent life, and his early poems burst through—under the sign of Novgorod, New York, or the Trans-Siberian Railway—not only the alexandrine meter, but to our chagrin they even exceed the length that would allow them to be taken up in an anthology! We console ourselves with three poems from the years 1913 to 1919, when Cendrars had established himself in Paris and took part not only in the avant-garde, but also in the events of the war: "Journal" (1913), harking back to the poem "Les Pâques," which had been written in New York one year before; "Les grands fétiches" (1916), with a view to the African art so esteemed by the Parisian avant-garde; and "Construction" (1919), with an eye to the artist Fernand Léger. The poems from Elisabeth Meylan and Niklaus Meienberg included here show that Cendrars also stepped over the boundary between French- and German-speaking Switzerland.

A half-century after Blaise Cendrars, in 1953, Nicolas Bouvier also set out into the wide world, traversing the Near, Middle, and Far East, and afterward wrote the travel narratives that have made him perhaps the most widely-read author in French-speaking Switzerland. To that renown, his letters and poems have made a notable contribution of their own.

Nicolas Bouvier left his homeland the same year as Philippe Jaccottet, likewise in order to explore the world. For this, however, Jaccottet had no need of a grand tour. He settled in Grignan, in southern France, where to this day he receives poets from all corners of the world and then sends them back out again in masterful translations. The poets of his native land also come and go, just as he himself always returns to them—returning home, so to speak. To this intimate relationship we owe what is probably the most beautiful collection of poems from the *Suisse romande*. In our anthology Jaccottet himself is not represented by verse, but rather by a prose poem. Surely no one will reproach us for considering prose in an anthology of lyric poems, as both Gustave Roud's "Sommeil" ("Sleep") and Jaccottet's "Les pivoines" ("Peonies") are more poetic than many a lyric.

Still, it is not given to everyone to be open to the world. Many poets from the *Suisse romande* feel themselves to be foreigners in their own country, their psychological and physical disposition coming into conflict with a conservative, primarily Protestant environment: Pierre-Louis Matthey opts first for the mask of the dandy, then isolation; Edmond-Henri Crisinel slips into depression, then suicide; Gustave Roud lives withdrawn on the parental farm, yet the surrounding Jorat becomes for him a surrogate world. So, too, do Maurice Chappaz and Corinna Bille, who spend the better part of their lives in the Valais, manage to create a universe out of their immediate environment. From Paris it may have looked as if they were living on the margin of the world, but from their own point of view they were at its center. And then there are those who are aware of the creative potential of the margins. Thus, Pierre Chappuis of Neuchâtel entitles one of his volumes of poetry *Pleines marges* (Full Margins). Whereas the margins there are bare and in our anthology are visible only as imagined emptiness, they are nevertheless full of significance. In the social world the marginal position may be a stigma, but in the poetic it can become a font of genuine lyric composition. The reader will also find such true poetry among the works of other poets of the *Suisse romande* collected here: Anne Perrier, Sylviane Dupuis, José-Flore Tappy, Jacques Chessex, Pierre-Alain Tâche, Pierre Voélin, Frédéric Wandelère, François Deblüe, and Claire Genoux.

Along with the canton of Ticino, Italophone Switzerland includes three valleys of the canton Graubünden, or the Grisons: the Misox, the Bergell, and the Puschlav. After a century of political, economic, and social upheavals that sapped all available energy—especially in the canton Ticino, which only became part of the Swiss Confederation in 1803—and so left hardly any room for lyric poetry whatever, a group, mainly of schoolteachers, recognized their calling at the start of the twentieth century and began to compose new poetry, along with stories and novels. Francesco Chiesa, Valerio Abbondio, and Giuseppe Zoppi have certainly achieved some renown, but in acknowledging their cultural merits, one must place them among the epigoni of the previous century's literature. It should not surprise us that none of them realized, or wanted to realize, that in parallel with their own efforts a dialect poetry was developing in Ticino that had no need to shy away from comparison with the poetry of "standard" Italian. On the contrary. Though it lacks the experimental character that sets the newer Swiss-German dialect poetry apart, the poems of a Giovanni Bianconi, Pino Bernasconi, Giovanni Orelli, or Elio Scamara, with their primal themes and richness of language, leave no reader unmoved. Nor should it surprise one that around the middle of the twentieth century, the modern poetry of Italy was neither assessed nor its significance appreciated by Chiesa or Abbondio, or even by Zoppi, who was then teaching as a professor of Italian Literature at the Federal Institute of Technology (ETH) in Zurich.

The Italian poets Giuseppe Ungaretti, Eugenio Montale, and Vittoria Sereni were introduced into Switzerland by Italian intellectuals living in exile, by Gianfranco Contini, who was teaching in Fribourg, and by a poet from Ticino who, as a twenty-three-year-old in 1944, published a little volume of poems, *Né bianco né viola* (Neither White Nor Purple), in which the archaic life of the upper Leventina in northern Ticino was unexpectedly merged with literary modernism: Giorgio Orelli. Orelli's feel for rhythm and sound, his encyclopedic and lexical curiosity, his stupendous erudition, the patience and care with which he prepares his volumes of poems and translations, make him a point of departure and lasting reference for contemporary poetry in Italophone Switzerland. All who came after—right up through Fabio Pusterla and Pietro de Marchi—are in one way or another in his debt; yet each—including Alberto Nessi, Aurelio Buletti, and Antonio Rossi—remains entirely his own poet, since Orelli's impact is not a matter of formulae, but of artistic scrupulousness. Already, Giorgio Orelli was looking—geographically and literarily—beyond the borders of his narrow homeland. With their poems about tortured animals on the way to the slaughterhouse and tortured humans in Bosnia, Fabio Pusterla and Vanni Bianconi, too, leave behind the realm of convention.

Joining the poets of canton Ticino in this volume are the poets of the Italophone Grisons—Remo Fasani, Felice Menghini, Grytzko Mascioni—as well as Donata Berra, and Pietro de Marchi, originally from Italy, and then the Modena-born university professor from Bern, Adolfo Jenni.

Unlike the French-, Italian-, and German-speaking regions of Switzerland, Rhaeto-Romania borders only countries where completely foreign languages are spoken. While authors from other parts of Switzerland live and write in the language and literature of the neighboring countries, the Romansh-speaking population are left, as it were, entirely on their own. Thus, even the oldest documents of Romansh culture were not written in a collective language. With the passage of time, five written languages have evolved in the different regions of the Grisons. Although at the turn of the last century a common language, the "Rumantsch Grischun," was created for practical use (official communications, legal texts, user instructions, etc.), up to the present day literature is still written primarily in the individual dialects—the idioms— of Rhaeto-Romania. All of these, save Sutsilvan, are represented in this volume: Vallader, the idiom of the Lower Engadine, by Peider Lansel, Andri Peer, Luisa Famos, Rut Plouda, Leta Semadeni, and Dumenic Andry; Puter, the idiom of the Upper Engadine, by Artur Caflisch and Göri Klainguti; Surmiran, the idiom of Oberhalbstein and the Albula valley, by Alexander Lozza; and Sursilvan, the idiom of the Vorderrhein valley, by Hendri Spescha, Vic Hendry, and Arno Camenisch.

Our Rhaeto-Romanic selection begins with Peider Lansel, the tireless champion of the renaissance of Romansh as a pure language, cleansed of German and Italian influences, and ends with Arno Camenisch, who drives renewal in the opposite direction, namely by mixing languages, and other games. His life as a "randulin" (in the Engandine one refers to commuters between the homeland and foreign territories as "swallows"), his collection of folk songs and other cultural artifacts, his polemics, and above all his poems make Peider Lansel an exemplary figure. He has not escaped the attention of a single one of his successors—and while some have gone no further than he, others have pressed for an even greater renewal of Romansh. Artur Caflisch, for one, poetically explores the characteristic sounds of his mother tongue, as does Andri Peer, who struggles against considerable local resistance to make a home for modern verse in Rhaeto-Romanic literature; he has translated T. S. Eliot, Montale, and also—to stay within the frame of our anthology—Werner Brambach and Maurice Chappaz. Giorgio Orelli has translated Peer, who dialogues with Albin Zollinger in "Dumengia in champogna" ("Sunday in the Country") as well as with Ovid, Baudelaire, and Valéry in "Furnatsch." But a true renewal of Romansh occurs wherever a poet descends into himself and into his language—when a Luisa Famos breathes new life into inherited themes and motifs, or when Vic Hendry, like Hendri Spescha before him, revives the short, short-lined poem, once frozen into cliché. Göri Klainguti and Dumenic Andry take a different approach: one of the most fascinating qualities of Romansh, in particular of the Puter and Vallader dialects, is the astonishing abundance of expletives. Klainguti has made this abundance the foundation of a story ("Gian Sulver"), Andry of a poem. The twenty-one lines of the first part of his "Tirada e retirada" ("A Rant & a Response"), consisting entirely of swear words, present any translator committed to literalism with an insoluble problem. Even German translators have discretely withdrawn and refrained from rendering a direct translation. Perhaps they wish thereby to invite the reader to compose his own version of the poem, fashioned from his own rich vocabulary. One should try! The length and number of lines matter little. Likewise, only free translation can do justice to the poems of Arno Camenisch, which stand in the tradition of non-sense verse. It should be made clear that in the original version of "Il tat ha ina vacca . . ." ("grandpa has a llama . . ."), the "auto mellen" ("yellow car"), seemingly absent from the English version, is also a reference to a kind of "non-sense," for the author hasn't here requisitioned a New York City taxi cab or a Swiss postal-service vehicle, but rather the ambulance of an insane asylum (hence its echo—as "gaga"—in the translation). For the two affecting poems by Artur Caflisch, which also play on sounds and words, the editor has provided his own English glosses.

Unlike the poets from the language regions toured above, the poets of German-speaking Switzerland could already look back to a rich tradition at the beginning of the twentieth century. Yet the heritage of a Gottfried Keller or a Conrad Ferdinand Meyer is also a burden from which many writers are not able to free themselves. Their whole lives—or poetic careers—they remain epigoni. Others, however, like Robert Walser or Gerhard Meier, search out their own voices with great humility; thanks to which they stand today alongside the literary giants of the past—but not alone.

Swiss-German literature of the past hundred years is rich in attempts to find new ways of moving poetry forward—and not only attempts, but successes (from the traditional, yet thoroughly idiosyncratic Albin Zollinger to the knowledgeable and multifaceted Elisabeth Meylan . . . or the ever-breathtaking Klaus Merz), and rich too in its struggle to create poetry from the stuff of life itself. Thus, Regina Ullmann's "Lebendes Bild" ("Tableau Vivant") is in fact wrung from life, a life spent first in special-needs schools, then in the literary worlds of Munich and Vienna, and after her expulsion from Germany, in a Catholic nursing home in St. Gallen. True, she converted from Judaism to Catholicism, but she would not allow herself to take the habit. In "Im Mohnfeld zur Gewitterszeit" ("A Poppy Field in the Middle of a Storm") she dons, instead, the red of that eponymous field—much as the robe of the Benedictine nun Silja Walter, in the early poem "Die Tänzerin" ("The Dancer"), also expands and comes to encompass the cosmic. In it rests "the meaning and the ways of things"—a roundelay of things, and certainly also of muses, as were later evoked in the poem "Il rudè" ("Ronde") by the Romansh poet Luisa Famos. But often, too—with Rainer Brambach, Alexander Xaver Gwerder, Adelheid Duvanel, or Niklaus Meienberg—life in the poem reveals itself as an existential affliction, as a personal affliction, or as the affliction of others.

The leap into modernity took place in German Switzerland in spectacular fashion, but it took many years for our poets to turn it into a glorious chapter for our literature: while the Swiss Frédéric-Louis Sauser (Blaise Cendrars) entered the ranks of the avant-garde in Paris, in Zurich the Germans Hans Arp, Hugo Ball, and Emmy Hennings set Dada in motion. In those days, Dada was scarcely noticed by many and by others only derided. Today

Dada is a subject of pride, and every Zurich city tour makes a stop in front of the Cabaret Voltaire. Some decades later, with his "concrete poems," Eugen Gomringer delineated another important precinct of modernism. But new forms and themes are also to be found in Felix Philipp Ingold, who in "Himmelskunde" ("Astronomy") and "Wetterkarte" ("Weather Map") charts heaven and earth—and language too—so as to reassemble them in the microcosm of the poem; much as in Urs Allemann's "Selbstporträt im Geäst" ("Self-Portrait in the Branches"); or in Rolf Hermann's "Hommage an das Rückenschwimmen in der Nähe von Chicago und Anderswo" ("An Homage to Backstroke Swimming Near Chicago and Elsewhere")—a poem as though conceived especially for this anthology. Lastly, in the sequence of poems "Manufakturen" ("Manufactures"), Raphael Urweider allows continents and seas (also sounds, letters, and words) to collide and drift apart, fixing them finally to twenty-four historical figures. Five of them, Magellan, Galileo, Gutenberg, Henry Ford, and Columbus, make appearances in our anthology. And then, all of a sudden—as if from another time, and yet timeless—Arnim Senser's "Grosses Erwachen" ("Great Awakening") awaits us.

Like its Italian counterpart, the German part of Switzerland is no stranger to poems in dialect, and they too stand comparison with poetry in the "standard" language. Our selection is limited to examples from the cantons of Bern and Valais: to the trailblazer Kurt Marti, as well as Albert Streich and Bernadette Lerjen-Sarbach, both set to music by Heinz Holliger. For copyright reasons, the poems of the songwriter Mani Matter, whose death in a fatal accident Marti commemorates in his diary poem "z.b. 25. 11. 72" ("e.g. 11/25/72"), have been omitted.

In homage to its host country, this anthology ends with a look forward and begins with a look back at America: namely, with the landing of Columbus in the so-called Indies and with the recollection of the poem "Les Pâques" by Blaise Cendrars, written in New York in 1912. Moreover, Robert Walser's intention to read, at long last, something by Proust is cited in homage to this anthology's place of publication. In the university library at Urbana-Champaign, he would have found ample opportunity.

Anyone who feels that this or that excluded poet, one or another overlooked theme or motif should absolutely have been included here, confirms my own heartfelt conclusion. Quite so: material for further volumes abounds.

My thanks go to the Max Geilinger Foundation, to Anne Marie Wells, President of the Translation House Looren Association, and to all those who made my road smoother: Bernd Jentzsch (*Schweizer Lyrik des zwanzigsten Jahrhunderts*, 1977), Roger Perret and Ingo Starz (*Wenn ich Schweiz sage . . . Schweizer Lyrik im Originalton von 1937 bis heute*, CD, 2010), Marion Graf and José-Flore Tappy (*La Poésie en Suisse Romande depuis Blaise Cendrars*, 2005), Philippe Jaccottet (*Die Lyrik der Romandie*, 2008), Giovanni Bonalumi, Renato Martinoni and Pier Vincenzo Menegaldo (*Cento anni di poesia nella Svizzera italiana*, 1997), Mevina Puorger (*Sbrinzlas = Funken = Scintille*, 2005), Dirk Vaihinger and Peter von Matt (*Die schönsten Gedichte der Schweiz*, 2002).

LUZIUS KELLER

MODERN AND CONTEMPORARY SWISS POETRY

I
FRENCH

TRANSLATED BY
JOHN TAYLOR

BLAISE CENDRARS

JOURNAL

Christ
Voici plus d'un an que je n'ai plus pensé à Vous
Depuis que j'ai écrit mon avant-dernier poème Pâques
Ma vie a bien changé depuis
Mais je suis toujours le même
J'ai même voulu devenir peintre
Voici les tableaux que j'ai faits et qui ce soir pendent aux murs
Ils m'ouvrent d'étranges vues sur moi-même qui me font penser
    à Vous.

Christ
La vie
Voilà ce que j'ai fouillé
Mes peintures me font mal
Je suis trop passionné
Tout est orangé.

J'ai passé une triste journée à penser à mes amis
Et à lire le journal
Christ

Vie crucifiée dans le journal grand ouvert que je tiens les bras tendus
Envergures
Fusées
Ébullition
Cris.
On dirait un aéroplane qui tombe.
C'est moi.

BLAISE CENDRARS

MY DAILY NEWS

Christ
More than a year's gone by since I've stopped thinking of You
Ever since I wrote my second-to-last poem Easter
My life has changed so much since then
But I'm still the same
I even wanted to become an artist
Here are the paintings I've made they're hanging on the walls tonight
Opening up strange views of myself and making me think
    of You.

Christ
It's life
I've rummaged through
My paintings hurt me
I'm too passionate
Everything is orange-colored.

I've spent a sad day thinking of my friends
And reading my daily news
Christ

Life crucified in my daily news that I hold out at arm's length
Wingspans
Rockets
Turmoil
Shouting.
Like an airplane crashing.
It's me.

Passion
Feu
Roman-feuilleton
Journal
On a beau ne pas vouloir parler de soi-même
Il faut parfois crier

Je suis l'autre
Trop sensible

Août 1913

LES GRANDS FÉTICHES

I

Une gangue de bois dur
Deux bras d'embryon
L'homme déchire son ventre
Et adore son membre dressé

II

Qui menaces-tu
Toi qui t'en vas
Poings sur les hanches
À peine d'aplomb
Juste hors de grossir?

Passion
Fire
Serial novel
My daily news
No matter how much you don't want to speak about yourself
Sometimes you have to shout

I'm the too sensitive
Other person

August 1913

THE GREAT FETISHES

I

Embedded in hard wood
Two embryo arms
The man tears at his stomach
And adores his erect prick

II

Who are you threatening
Strutting off like that
Fists on your haunches
Barely back on your feet
After giving birth?

III

Nœud de bois
Tête en forme de gland
Dur et réfractaire
Visage dépouillé
Jeune dieu insexué et cyniquement hilare

IV

L'envie t'a rongé le menton
La convoitise te pipe
Tu te dresses
Ce qui te manque du visage
Te rend géométrique
Arborescent
Adolescent

V

Voici l'homme et la femme
Également laids également nus
Lui moins gras qu'elle mais plus fort
Les mains sur le ventre et la bouche en tire-lire

VI

Elle
Le pain de son sexe qu'elle fait cuire trois fois par jour
Et la pleine outre du ventre
Tirent
Sur le cou et les épaules

III

A wooden knot
A head like a prick
Or tough hard acorn
Yet bland-faced and sexless
This cynically hilarious young god

IV

Craving has chewed your chin away
Lust gives you a suck
You prick up
What your face lacks
Makes you geometric
Treelike
A teenager

V

Look at the man and the woman
Equally ugly equally naked
He's less fat than her yet stronger
His hands on his stomach and his mouth like a piggy bank

VI

That woman
With the bread of her sex that she cooks three times a day
And the bloated bota bag of her stomach
Pulling down
On her neck and shoulders

VII

Je suis laid!
Dans ma solitude à force de renifler l'odeur des filles
Ma tête enfle et mon nez va bientôt tomber

VIII

J'ai voulu fuir les femmes du chef
J'ai eu la tête fracassée par la pierre du soleil
Dans le sable
Il ne reste plus que ma bouche
Ouverte comme le vagin de ma mère
Et qui crie

IX

Lui
Chauve
N'a qu'une bouche
Un membre qui descend aux genoux
Et les pieds coupés

X

Voici la femme que j'aime le plus
Deux rides aiguës autour d'une bouche en entonnoir
Un front bleu
Du blanc sur les tempes
Et le regard astiqué comme un cuivre

British Museum,
Londres, février 1916

VII

I'm ugly!
And sniff girlish scents in my solitude so often
My head is swelling and my nose is ready to drop off

VIII

I wanted to flee all the chief's wives
The stone of the sun smashed my head apart
Right here in the sand
Only my mouth is left
Gaping like my mother's vagina
And screaming

IX

He's
Bald
Has got only one mouth
A dick that droops to his knees
And cut-off feet

X

Here's the woman I love the most
Two wrinkles slash around her funnel-mouth
Her forehead is blue
Her temples are white
And her gaze is polished like copper

British Museum,
London, February 1916

CONSTRUCTION

De la couleur, de la couleur et des couleurs . . .
Voici Léger qui grandit comme le soleil de l'époque tertiaire
Et qui durcit
Et qui fixe
La nature morte
La croûte terrestre
Le liquide
Le brumeux
Tout ce qui se ternit
La géométrie nuageuse
Le fil à plomb qui se résorbe
Ossification.
Locomotion.
Tout grouille
L'esprit s'anime soudain et s'habille à son tour comme
    les animaux et les plantes
Prodigieusement
Et voici
La peinture devient cette chose énorme qui bouge
La roue
La vie
La machine
L'âme humaine
Une culasse de 75
Mon portrait

Février 1919

CONSTRUCTION

Color, color, and colors . . .
Here's Léger growing like the sun of the tertiary
And hardening
And stabilizing
The still life
The earth's crust
Liquidness
Haziness
All that tarnishes
Cloudy geometry
The plumb line drawing itself back up
Ossification.
Locomotion.
Everything swarming
The spirit suddenly coming to life and dressing like
    animals and plants
Prodigiously
And thus
Painting becomes that enormous thing that moves
The wheel
Life
The machine
The human soul
A French 75
My portrait

February 1919

PIERRE-LOUIS MATTHEY

SONATE DE L'INDIGNE AVEU

Qu'il se le dise! Ô le soleil est son aïeul
Le ciel sa confidente et les oiseaux ses frères . . .
Mais qu'il garde l'aveu qui enflamme ses lèvres:
Au cœur de son silence il est encore ouï.

Le vois-tu sous la lampe? Ô front que rien ne baise,
Ô poursuite des yeux qui trouvent tout de pierre
Se débattant toujours dans la même lumière
Comme une île impuissante à sortir de sa mer.

Il lève vers son ombre une bouche adorable
Et qui ne s'est livrée à des lèvres qu'en rêve,
Et qui rêve toujours de quelque baiser grave
Telle une fleur toujours hantée de son parfum . . .

Qu'il se le dise! Ô le soleil est son aïeul
Le ciel sa confidente et les oiseaux ses frères . . .
Mais qu'il garde l'aveu qui enflamme ses lèvres:
Silence est la vertu du coupable chanteur.

Il a vu lentement la lune se parfaire
Et lentement les fruits mûrir le long des mois . . .
Son seul bonheur serait de partager sa vie:
Il lui sera permis quelque jour . . . il le croit.

Il a vu des blessés. Il hait celui qui blesse.
C'est guérir qu'il voudrait, ni meurtrir, ni blesser . . .
Il blesserait, il le sait trop, et sa faiblesse,
S'il ne serrait les lèvres, hélas, cet inbaisé.

SONATA OF THE SHAMEFUL AVOWAL

Let him proclaim it! The sun is his grandfather
The sky his confidante and the birds his brothers . . .
But let him keep back the avowal burning his lips:
At the heart of his silence it can still be heard.

Do you see him bent under his lamp? O unkissed forehead,
O darting eyes spotting everything as stone
And ever struggling in the same cone of light
Like an impotent island trapped in its sea.

He lifts toward the other man's shadow a lovely mouth
That has given itself over to lips only in dreams
And that ever dreams of some solemn kiss
And that is flowerlike, ever haunted by his fragrance . . .

Let him proclaim it! The sun is his grandfather
The sky his confidante and the birds his brothers . . .
But let him keep back the avowal burning his lips:
Silence is the virtue of the guilty singer.

He has seen the moon slowly filling out
And watched the fruit ripening as the months go by . . .
His only happiness would be sharing his life:
He will be allowed to some day . . . so he believes.

He has seen the wounded. He hates him who wounds.
He would rather heal, not bruise, nor wound . . .
But he would wound, he knows, as does his weakness,
If he, never once kissed, alas, loosened his lips.

Et s'il parle de soi comme on fait d'un autre homme
Pour être moins tenté de se soudain trahir,
Il implore humblement que chacun lui pardonne
Ce vêtement d'orgueil qu'aussitôt il déchire.

And if he speaks about himself as if about another man
To be less tempted to go and give himself away,
He humbly begs everyone to forgive him
For this haughty garment he suddenly tears to pieces.

EDMOND-HENRI CRISINEL

ÉLÉGIE DE LA MAISON DES MORTS

À Gérard Buchet

I

Château bordé de calme et de feuillage épars . . .
C'est ici le séjour de la Mélancolie!
De ces nobles bosquets la chaîne est un rempart
Où vient mourir l'écho de tes crimes, Folie!

Passant, la grille est close et le soir tombe. Va!
Tu ne comprendrais pas ce qui tourmente et ronge.
Dans leur trouble sommeil les ombres d'ici-bas.
Maison des morts—îlot perdu—débris de songe.

II

Dans ces lieux inhumains, flamme et glace! j'ai vu
Les victimes des dieux fuir la Meute hurlante;
À leur passé défunt le corps a survécu,
Mais leurs yeux sont fermés sur des taches sanglantes.

Comme elles, j'ai maudit le jour où je suis né,
Sous tes mâchicoulis, tour antique et bannie;
Comme elles, pourchassé d'ombres, j'ai frissonné
D'entendre vos clameurs, ô mâles Érinnyes!

EDMOND-HENRI CRISINEL

ELEGY OF THE HOUSE OF THE DEAD

To Gérard Buchet

I

A chateau edged with quiet and scattered woods . . .
This is the very spot where Melancholy dwells!
From these noble groves the mountains raise their ramparts
Against which die the echo of your crimes, Insanity!

The iron-rail gate is closed, stroller, night is falling. Leave!
You wouldn't understand what torments, gnaws away
At earthly shades writhing in their fitful sleep.
House of the dead—lost isle—debris of dream.

II

In these inhuman parts, flame and ice! I've seen
The victims of gods fleeing the bellowing Pack;
Their bodies have outlived their buried past,
But their eyes stay shut to all the bloody stains.

Like them, I cursed the day when I was born
Under your machicolation, ancient banished tower;
Like them, pursued by shades, I shivered
When hearing your shouts, O male Erinyes!

III

Quand le soir est trop lourd d'angoisse, quand le miel
Du jasmin dans la nuit vous oppresse, on s'évade.
Mais les murs sont trop hauts. Ils montent jusqu'au ciel.
On reste prisonnier, pour toujours, dans la rade.

Calme, breuvage amer, cet excès de douleur.
Ô lumière ennemie! et vous, roses parterres!
Sachant que, jamais plus, la fleur ne sera fleur,
Par delà les œillets je regarde la terre.

IV

"Une ombre bien-aimée est au fond de vos yeux,
Comme au fond de mes yeux, amantes délaissées . . .
Nous l'avons oubliée, et, dit-elle, c'est mieux.
Mais plus ne dormirons, nébuleuses blessées."

Dans la maison des morts une femme chantait,
Jusqu'à l'aube chantait, jamais lasse, obstinée.
Du pays détesté les gouffres se rouvraient.
Elle éveillait les morts. Un soir, ils l'ont tuée.

III

When anguish lades the evening, when the honey
Of the jasmine suffocates you at night, you flee.
But the walls rise too high. All the way to heaven.
And forever you stay a stranded prisoner in the bay.

Do calm, bitter beverage, this excess pain.
O enemy light, and you, pink flowerbeds!
Knowing no flower will ever again be flower,
I gaze at the dirt beyond the carnation beds.

IV

"A beloved shade lurks deeply in your eyes,
As in mine, abandoned lovers. . .
We've forgotten her and, she adds, it's better.
But no longer will we sleep, wounded nebulae."

In the house of the dead would sing a woman,
Sing until dawn, never weary, obstinate.
The hated country's chasms once again would open.
She would wake the dead. One evening, they killed her.

V

Avez-vous entendu, vers minuit, ce soupir?
Mains jointes, bras en croix pour une mort absente . . .
M'avez-vous entendu, harpes du ciel, gémir?
Voix maudites, assez! ma vie est innocente!

Quand l'Ange m'a laissé, blême, sur les tapis,
Le jour, hélas! peut-il blesser des yeux plus vagues?
Si, dans les champs, demain, vous glanez des épis,
Femmes, fuyez ce fou qui se signe et divague.

VI

Ô vous, corps oubliés dans vos humbles cercueils,
Le front bas, j'ai les voûtes infernales,
Mais vos râles, vos cris, vos transes, comme un deuil,
Ont égaré mes pas dans l'ombre sépulcrale.

Ainsi, Dieu m'a rouvert, dans vos cités, vivants,
Ce sillage où je puise au trésor du silence.
Quelques secrets, ravis à la nuit des grands vents,
M'ont laissé des lueurs dont vit mon espérance.

V

Did you hear, near midnight, a stint of sighing?
Hands clasped, arms outstretched for one who's dead
And not yet here . . . Heavenly harps, did you hear me moaning?
Enough of this, damned voices! My life is innocent!

When the Angel left me pallid on the carpets,
The daylight, alas! Can it wound still duller eyes?
Women, if in the fields tomorrow you glean the wheat,
Run from this raving lunatic who crosses himself.

VI

And you, corpses, left to your humble coffins,
My forehead bowed, I too have the hellish vaults,
And your gasps, your cries, your trances, like mourning,
Have misled my steps among the sepulchral shadows.

And you, the living, God has opened in your towns
This wake in which I draw on silence's wealth,
While secrets stolen from the night of mighty winds,
Have left me glimmers nourishing my hopes.

GUSTAVE ROUD

SOMMEIL

Pas de paroles solennelles, nul cri près de cet homme qui dort au
centre du monde, sur la plus haute des collines. Voyez comme il
est simple et las! Les seigles sont fauchés. Il a jeté sa faux ternie
par le trèfle et la terre; il s'est couché, sa force dénouée comme
une gerbe. Il dort. Bleu-de-ciel, brun-de-seigle; tout bleu des pieds
à l'étroite ceinture de cuir, puis jusqu'aux cheveux sombres, plus
fauve que la moisson abattue. Couleur de terre, couleur de ciel;
dans son vêtement et sa chair réconciliant terre et ciel; lieu de
chair où s'opère enfin leur communion profonde. Ce corps puis-
sant déborde de toutes parts son ombre, offert comme sur un autel
parmi le peuple des collines prosternées sous leur vêture de fro-
ment dans la fournaise, jusqu'à la neige pure des montagnes. Vie
suspendue, ô corps abandonné, qui donc de toute éternité m'avait
choisi pour conduire les hommes se pencher à travers les siècles
sur votre sommeil?
   C'est un moissonneur qui dort au midi d'août dans l'herbe flé-
trie. Caressé par le vent, caressé par la glissante ombre des nuages
plus hauts que le soleil, caressé par les cloches de midi que le feu
de cent clochers roule comme une fumée sur le monde, homme
de toute éternité choisi pour être celui qui *est,* en qui terre et ciel
se complaisent parce qu'en eux il s'est complu. La terre le donne
au ciel, à l'extrême de sa colline la plus pure, la première visitée
par l'aurore. Aimé!, laissez-moi lui donner son nom; que soit dite
une fois au moins la salutation attendue! Et mon devoir me sera
remis.
   Couché dans l'herbe et les fleurs refleuries, près du feu de la
faux, du rouge coffin renversé, la joue serrée au repli de l'énorme
bras de bronze, lèvres ouvertes . . . La fatigue fait saillir par instant

GUSTAVE ROUD

SLEEP

No solemn words, no shouting near this man sleeping at the center of the world, on the highest hill. See how simple and weary he is! The rye has been reaped. He has tossed aside his scythe tarnished by the clover and the dirt; he has lain down, his energy fallen apart like a sheaf. He is sleeping. Sky blue, rye brown; all blue from his feet up to the narrow leather belt, then from there to his dark hair, more fawn-colored than the threshed harvest. Earth color, sky color; in his clothes and in his flesh reconciling earth and sky; flesh in which their deep communion at last occurs. Every part of his powerful body extends beyond its shadow and is offered as if on an altar among the people of the hills who are bowed down, clothed in wheat, amid the blazing heat and all the way up to the pure snow of the mountains. Suspended life, O abandoned body: who, then, has chosen me from the beginning of time to lead human beings to where they can bend, across the centuries, over your sleep?

He is a harvester sleeping at high noon in August on the withered grass. Caressed by the wind, caressed by the slippery shadow of clouds higher than the sun, caressed by the noon bells that the fire of a hundred steeples rolls out like smoke over the world, this man from the beginning of time who has been chosen to be he who *is*, in whom earth and sky revel because it is in them that he revels. The earth offers him to the sky, at the highest point of its purest hill, the first visited by the dawn. Aimé! Let me give him his name; may the expected greeting be pronounced at least once! And my duty will be accomplished.

Lying in the grass and the reblooming flowers, near the fire of the scythe and the turned-over red whetstone holder, his cheek tucked away in the bend of his big bronze arm, his lips open . . .

le frisson d'un muscle sous la peau nue. L'épaule écrase un jet de campanules. Ô vraiment fils de la terre, humblement, doucement porté par elle, Aimé, cerné de ses fleurs, rafraîchi de ses fruits (tes lèvres noircies des dernières cerises)—mais saisi plus encore par le ciel! C'est lui que de l'aube au soir tu portes à tes épaules, qui flotte à tes deux poings comme une bannière de soie! Le souffle que ta gorge aspire, expire est si juste, sa mesure tellement parfaite que le ciel oublie en son sein le musical glissement d'étoiles par myriades; il songe à ton regard où il habite, clair prisonnier de l'humain; il veut surprendre dans ton cœur l'écho vivant de son propre cœur. Il se penche si doucement sur toi que rien ne peut rompre ton repos, pas même l'immense tête bleue qui s'abat sans bruit sur ta poitrine, comme une femme.

Out of tiredness a muscle shivers at times under the naked skin. His shoulder crushes a spray of bellflowers. O truly a son of the earth you are, Aimé, humbly, softly borne by it, surrounded by its flowers, freshened by its fruits (your lips blackened by the last cherries)—but hugged even more by the sky! It's the sky that you bear on your shoulders from dawn to evening, that flutters like a silk banner on your two fists! The breath that your throat inhales, exhales, is so exact, its tempo so perfect, that the sky forgets the myriads of stars musically gliding through its bosom; it dreams of your gaze where it dwells, a clear prisoner of human beings; it wants to overhear the living echo of its own heart, in your heart. It bends so softly over you that nothing can upset your sleep, not even the immense blue head, which, like a woman, noiselessly smashes down on your chest.

MAURICE CHAPPAZ

LE VALAIS AU GOSIER DE GRIVE (*extraits*)

I

Le Valais de bois est à l'agonie.
Le Valais qui est la seule parcelle de l'Éden,
dans une fente de neige
entre les siècles dormants
hostie intacte et fraîche.

Valais de l'abîme!
Aux joues brunes, aux reins de forêts bleues,
beurrées par le fœhn.
Les hommes enfoncés comme des clous de souliers.

Légion de collines, de calvaires,
de pics, de vallées de Josaphat;
et le lit du fleuve
taciturne.

Cette force qu'il y a dans les doigts d'artistes forcenés,
d'accoucheurs à bloc qui ont pincé du rocher
le rameau total de la vigne.

Et leurs boyaux comme des orvets,
les Jean petit Jean et les Marie Maria ont rampé
et ont enfanté du marécage
des millions d'arbres fruitiers.

MAURICE CHAPPAZ

from THRUSH-THROATED VALAIS

I

Woody Valais is at its last dying gasps.
Valais the sole parcel of Eden,
in a crack in the snowbank
between the slumbering centuries,
a fresh and intact holy wafer.

Abysmal Valais!
With its brown cheeks, its kidneys of blue forests
buttered by the foehn.
Men hammered in like shoe tacks.

A legion of hills, roadside crosses,
peaks, Valleys of Jehoshaphat;
and the bed of the
taciturn river.

The forceful fingers of those frenzied artists,
baby deliverers who bent over boulder-like slopes
and pinched out every single vinestock from the rock.

And their guts like slowworms,
The Johns Li'l Johns Maries and Marias who crawled
and gave birth from the swamp
to millions of fruit trees.

Cette force qu'il y a dans la bouche et qui s'est toujours tue
et ne s'est ouverte que pour les psaumes et les prophètes
latins et patois.
Cette voix d'orgue et d'harmonica.

Le grain qu'on ne peut moudre;
leurs dents blanches.
Le vin de sang et de muscat.

Au commencement étaient les grands Christ paysans.

VIII

Ce sol est macération de verger et de désert,
éruption de la foudre et de l'abricot.

Voici les paysannes à bustes d'évêques,
chacune une église du Christ incarné.
Il a souffert,
elles aussi!
Puis le Valais l'apôtre neuf,
le pur-sang trapu,
vibre dans une mandorle de moteurs.
Bougre de bon!

Je suis leur enfant,
au fond de moi
un cri de martre.
Le Verbe, telle une dent de lait
vient de percer.

This force filling the mouth and that has always kept silent,
opening only for psalms
and Latin or patois prophets.
This organ and harmonica voice.

The seed that can't be ground;
their white teeth.
The wine of blood and Muscat grapes.

In the beginning were big peasant Christs.

VIII

This ground is a maceration of orchard and desert,
an eruption of lightning bolts and apricots.

Look at these peasant women with their bishop chests,
every one of them a church of Christ incarnate.
He suffered,
so did they!
And now Valais the brand new apostle,
the thickset thoroughbred,
vibrates in a mandorla of motors.
A splendid fellow!

I am their child,
deep inside myself
a marten squeals.
The Word, like a milk tooth
has just cut through the gum.

CORINNA BILLE

LES RAISINS DE VERRE

Je suis entrée un jour dans une chapelle de ce Haut-Valais si sombre, si cruel, que je dus tenir mon cœur à deux mains.

Les voûtes étaient basses et les saintes exsangues dans leurs cercueils de verre. Toute affaiblie, je dus m'assoir et je m'endormis.

À mon réveil je me vis prisonnière. Des colonnes torses de l'autel, la vigne avait poussé jusqu'à moi. Ses vrilles serraient ma taille, les pampres verdâtres pesaient sur mon crâne et quant je voulus approcher mes lèvres sèches de leurs grappes glauques, troubles—avec la pruine des myrrhes accumulées—, je sentis craquer sous ma dent les raisins de verre.

L'ŒIL SULFATE

C'était l'aurore.

La fenêtre grillagée donnait sur la vigne, une vigne aussi haute qu'une forêt.

Je regardais les feuilles couvertes de sulfate.

Au centre de chacune d'elles s'ouvrait un œil, un œil bleu-vert comme les feuilles.

Je pris mon fusil de chasse et je tirais sur les yeux, les yeux bleu-vert comme les feuilles.

Il n'y eut plus alors que des trous noirs et ce fut la Mort qui me regarda.

CORINNA BILLE

THE GLASS GRAPES

One day I entered a chapel in this Haut-Valais region, so dark and cruel that I had to clutch my heart with both hands.

The vaulted ceiling was low and the saints were bloodless in their glass coffins. Faint and feeble, I had to sit down. I fell asleep.

Upon awakening, I saw I was a prisoner. From the wreathed columns of the altar the grapevine had grown all the way over to me. Its tendrils were wrapping tightly around my waist, the greenish vine branches were weighing down on my skull and when I approached my dry lips to their murky blue-green clusters—with the waxy bloom of the accumulated myrrh—I felt the glass grapes cracking under my teeth.

THE SULFATE EYE

It was daybreak.

The chicken-wire-covered window looked out on the vineyard, whose vines rose as high as a forest.

I was looking at the leaves covered with sulfate.

In the middle of each one an eye was opening, a blue-green eye like the leaves.

I took my hunting rifle and shot at the eyes, those blue-green eyes like the leaves.

Now there was nothing left but black holes and it was Death gazing at me.

ANNE PERRIER

AIRS GRECS (*extraits*)

Si j'avais un jardin
Vaste comme la rêverie
Je m'en irais dormir au fond des giroflées
Dormir mourir
Dans le balancement des âges
Et le monde comme un cerceau
Continuerait sa course sur l'abîme
Astre fantôme jouet d'enfants
Aux yeux bandés

*

Couronnée d'oiseaux
La mort quand viendra-t-elle
Me tendre la fleur d'églantier
L'heure monte au zénith
La coupe du silence est pleine
À peine entend-on battre
À ma tempe le sang
Ce voyageur qui ralentit le pas
Au bord de l'ineffable

*

Désormais chaque année
Est une rose extrême dans un vase
Près de se briser

ANNE PERRIER

from GREEK AIRS

If I had a garden
Vast like reverie
Off I'd go to sleep deep in the gillyflowers
To sleep to die
Rocked by the ages
And the world like a casket
Would keep rushing to the abyss
A phantom star a toy
For children with blindfolds

*

Crowned with birds
When will death come
To hand me a wild rose
The hour soars to the zenith
The cup of silence is full
The blood beating in my temples
Can barely be heard
Like a traveler slowing down
At the edge of the ineffable

*

From now on every year
There is an extreme rose in a vase
Ready to shatter

PHILIPPE JACCOTTET

LES PIVOINES

Elles n'ont pas duré.

Tout juste le temps d'être de petites balles, de petits globes lisses et denses, quelques jours; puis, cédant à une poussée intérieure, de s'ouvrir, de se déchiffonner, comme autant d'aubes autour d'un poudroiement doré de soleil.
Comme autant de robes, si l'on veut. Si vous y incite l'insistante rêverie.

Opulentes et légères, ainsi que certains nuages.

Une explosion relativement lente et parfaitement silencieuse.

La grâce dérobée des fleurs.

Parce qu'elles s'inclinent sous leur propre poids, certaines jusqu'à terre, on dirait qu'elles vous saluent, quand on voudrait les avoir soi-même, le premier, saluées.

Ainsi groupées, on dirait une figure de ballet.

Comme *la Danse* de Carpeaux, devant l'Opéra (du moins le souvenir qui m'en revient), les unes tournées vers le ciel, d'autres vers la terre.

PHILIPPE JACCOTTET

THE PEONIES

They have not lasted.

Just enough time—a few days—to exist as little balls; as small, sleek, dense globes; then, obeying an inner impulse, to open up, to smooth themselves out, like so many dawns around golden powdery suns.

Like so many gowns, if you will. If the insistent daydream incites you to such a simile.

Light and opulent, like certain clouds.

A relatively slow, perfectly silent explosion.

The stealthy grace of flowers.

Because they bow under their own weight, some of them all the way to the ground, they seem to greet you when you wish you had greeted them first.

Grouped together, they look like a ballet figure.

Like the women in Carpeaux's *Dance* in front of the Opera (at least as I remember it now): some of them turned toward the sky, the others toward the earth.

Pour les saisir, il faut s'en éloigner.

Que verra-t-on, alors? Une figure dessinée sur le miroir par la buée? Un jeu de balles?

Je vous salue, arbuste plein de grâce.

Mais revoici une fois de plus le vieil homme, avec ou sans complice, épiant Suzanne à travers quelque haie! Je le voyais venir, d'autant que ce n'est pas tout à fait arbitraire: un regard un peu troublé comme l'est le sien, le leur, peut bien s'imaginer surprendre là une figure de ballet, entre mousse et satin, avec la révérence finale, jusqu'à terre, le salut qui vaut aussi pour vous, après tout, rêveurs perclus!

Mais le rideau tombe vite, toujours trop vite, quelles qu'aient été la grâce des saluts, la chaleur des applaudissements. Et vous vous retrouvez un peu plus voûtés, un peu plus frileux, dans la rue noire.

(Ce vieil homme, avec ou sans complice, on pourrait le suivre, au retour de pareille soirée, jusque chez lui; décrire, minutieusement ou non, son logis, où la solitude irrémédiable fait passer un courant d'air froid même aux plus beaux jours de l'année; raconter comment il se défend contre l'absence d'espoir, la fatigue, le souci, par quelles inventions ingénieuses ou naïves; de quelles frêles barrières il s'entoure, repoussant ainsi, avec une touchante patience, l'avance du froid qui le menace, alors même qu'il sait n'avoir aucune chance de gagner. Ces choses-là peuvent et ont pu être dites, ne serait-ce que pour rendre hommage à la vaillance humaine; ou, au contraire, pour dénoncer la cruauté, la monstruosité de l'ennemi qui a tant de noms et n'en a aucun. Mais je préfère décidément jouer le valet presque invisible qui suspend encore dans les feuillages ces quelques lanternes de papier blanc et rose, comme si l'on pouvait encore aujourd'hui fêter une fête, même une fête des morts, dans ce monde vermoulu.)

To grasp them, you have to move away.

What will you see, then? A figure drawn by breath on the mirror? A ball game?

I greet you, graceful shrub.

But here once again is the old man, with or without an accomplice, spying on Suzanne through a hedge! I knew he would show up, for this is not mere happenstance: a rather distraught look like his, or theirs, can well imagine chancing upon a ballet figure here, amid tulle and satin, with the final bow all the way to the ground, after all, being a farewell also destined for you, crippled dreamers! But the curtain falls quickly, always too quickly, however graceful the farewells, however warm the applause. And you find yourselves a little more hunched over, and shivering a little more, in the black street.

(You could follow this old man, with or without an accomplice, as he returned home from such an evening; describe, in minute detail or not, his lodgings where irremediable solitude lets in chilly drafts even on the mildest days of the year; tell how he defends himself— through whatever ingenious or ingenuous inventions—against weariness, worry, a lack of hope; how he surrounds himself with whatever fragile barriers, thereby staving off, with touching patience, the onslaught of the cold threatening him, although he knows that he has no chance of winning. Such things can be and could have been said, if only in tribute to human valor; or, on the contrary, to denounce the cruelty and monstrosity of an enemy that has many names, and none. But I obviously prefer taking on the role of the nearly invisible valet who still hangs these few white and pink paper lanterns in the foliage, as if it were still possible to celebrate some festival today, even a festival of the dead, in this worm-eaten world.)

Les voyeurs bénins abandonnés à leur mélancolique obsession, verra-t-on plus clair qu'ils ne l'ont fait? Faudra-t-il, pour cela, plus d'attention ou plus d'insouciance? Plus, ou moins de détours? Sûrement, plus d'ingénuité.

Opulentes, épanouies et légères à la manière de certains nuages (qui ne sont, après tout, que de la pluie encore en ballot, tenue en main); de nuages arrêtés, sans s'effilocher, dans les feuilles.

Pas plus nuages, néanmoins, que robes déchiffonnées: pivoines, et qui se dérobent, qui vous échappent—dans un autre monde, à peine lié au vôtre.

C'est la plus ancienne fleur dont je garde le souvenir, dans le jardin, encore vaguement visible, de très loin: fleur pesante, mouillée, comme une joue contre mon genou d'enfant, dans l'enclos de hauts murs et de buis taillés.

Cela se fripe vite, devient vite jaunâtre et mauve, comme de vieilles lettres d'amour dans un roman à la Werther.

Une passion sans lendemain, rien qu'une rougeur aperçue à travers un rideau de joncs tels qu'on en installe aux premières mouches de l'été.

(Comme on dit volontiers: "tout cela est bien beau, mais encore? . . . ")

Will we ever see more clearly than these harmless voyeurs given over to their melancholy obsession? For this to happen, will we need to be more attentive or carefree? To take more, or fewer, side-tracks? Certainly, we will need to be more ingenuous.

Opulent, in full bloom, yet light like some clouds (which, after all, are mere bundled rain held in a hand); unfraying clouds held in check amid leaves.

Actually, neither clouds nor smoothed-out gowns: they are peonies, and they steal away, slip away from you—into another world, barely linked to yours.

It is the oldest flower that I recall; still vaguely visible from far off, in the garden: a heavy moist flower like a cheek against my infant knee, within the enclosure with its high walls and trimmed boxwood.

They quickly crumple, become mauve and yellowish, like old love letters in a *Werther*-like novel.

A passion with no future, merely a redness spotted through one of those cane curtains that you hang across doors when the first summer flies appear.

(As one readily says: "All this is just fine, but what now? . . .")

Elles n'auront pas longtemps orné ce coin de jardin.

Pourquoi donc y a-t-il des fleurs?

Elles s'ouvrent, elles se déploient, comme on voudrait que le fassent le temps, notre pensée, nos vies.

L'ornement, l'inutile, le dérobé.

Saluez ces plantes, pleines de grâce.

Parure, vivante, brièveté changée en parure, fragilité faite parure.

Avec ceci de particulier, sinon de plus, qu'elles pèsent, qu'elles s'inclinent, comme trop lasses pour porter leur charge de couleur. Quelques gouttes de pluie et ce serait l'éparpillement, la défaite, la chute.

Plus je me donne de mal, et bien que ce soit à leur gloire, plus elles se retranchent dans un monde inaccessible. Non qu'elles soient farouches, ou moqueuses, ou coquettes! Elles ne veulent pas qu'on parle à leur place. Ni qu'on les couvre d'éloges, ou les compare à tout et à rien; au lieu de, tout bonnement, les montrer.
C'est encore trop que d'écrire qu'elles ne veulent pas, ou veulent quoi que ce soit. Elles habitent un autre monde en même temps que celui d'ici; c'est pourquoi justement elles vous échappent, vous obsèdent. Comme une porte qui serait à la fois, inexplicablement, entrouverte et verrouillée.

They will not long have ornamented this corner of the garden.

Why then do flowers exist?

They open, they unfold, as we wish time, our thoughts, our lives would do.

Ornamentation, uselessness, what steals away.

Greet these graceful plants.

Living finery, brevity turned into finery, frailness made into finery.

With this in particular, if not in addition: that they are heavy, that they bow down, as if too weary to bear their burden of color. A few raindrops, and the dispersal, the undoing, the downfall would ensue.

The more trouble I take, and although it is to their glory, the further they withdraw into an inaccessible world. Not that they are shy, or scoffing, or coquettish! They do not want anyone to speak up for them. Nor to cover them with praise or compare them to anything and everything; instead of pointing to them, simply enough.

It is even too much to write that they "do not want," or "want" anything at all. They dwell in another world at the same time as this one; this is precisely why they slip away from you, obsess you. Like a door that would be, inexplicably, both half-open and bolted shut.

N'empêche que, s'il fallait passer par une ressemblance avec autre chose qu'elles, la plus juste serait, pour chacune, avec une aube, avec un épanouissement de rose et de blanc autour du pollen, du poudroiement doré du soleil, comme si elles étaient chargées d'en garder mémoire, d'en multiplier les preuves, d'en rafraîchir le sens.

Je ne sais quoi, qui n'est pas seulement un souvenir d'enfance, les accorde avec la pluie. Avec une voûte, une arche de verdure. Elles vont ensemble: est-ce à cause des nuages?

Avant que n'approche la pluie, je vais à la rencontre des pivoines.

Elles n'auront pas duré.

Approchées, même pas dans la réalité de telle journée de mars, rien que dans la rêverie, elles vous précèdent, elles poussent des portes de feuilles, de presque invisibles barrières. On va les suivre, sous des arceaux verts; et que l'on se retourne, peut-être s'apercevra-t-on que l'on ne fait plus d'ombre, que vos pas ne laissent plus de traces dans la boue.

All the same, if you had to seek out a resemblance to something other than what they are, the most accurate one, for each peony, would be a dawn; an unfolding of pink and white around pollen, around the golden powdery sun, as if they were responsible for preserving the memory of this, for offering proof of it time and again, for refreshing its meaning.

I do not know what it is, beyond mere childhood memories, that puts peonies into harmony with the rain. With a vault, an archway of greenery. They go together: is this because of clouds?

Before the rain approaches, I go to meet the peonies.

They will not have lasted.

Once approached—not even in the reality of a March day, but in a mere daydream—they go before you, pushing open leafy doors, almost invisible barriers. You are going to follow them, beneath the green arches; and if you look back, perhaps you will see that no shadow is cast behind you, that your steps leave no more tracks in the mud.

NICOLAS BOUVIER

LOVE SONG I

Un peu de gris, un peu de pluie
et c'en est déjà presque trop
il faut chanter si bas pour t'endormir
Circé du bord des larmes

frêle et fragile comme tu l'es
parfois je me demande
d'où te viennent ces larges richesses d'ombre
et dans quels jeux silencieux tu t'égares
avec cette soie dévidée dans le noir
sans doute ne sais-tu pas toi-même
pour quelle lumière inconcevable
tu as préparé tant de nuit

Auberge aveugle du chagrin
ouverte et jamais pleine
mon beau bémol
ma douce haine

ton secret, tes couloirs
tes veines
où j'habite et retiens ma voix.

Nakano-ku, Tokyo, février 1965

NICOLAS BOUVIER

LOVE SONG I

A little gray, a little rain
and it's almost already too much
so softly I have to sing you to sleep
Circe on the brink of tears

frail and fragile as you are
sometimes I wonder how this vast
shadowy wealth came to you
and in what silent games you go astray
with this silk unwound in the darkness
you yourself probably don't know
for what inconceivable light
you've prepared so much night

Blind inn of sorrow
open and never full
my beautiful B-flat doubt
my sweet hatred

your secret, your hallways
your veins
in which I live and withhold my voice.

Nakano-ku, Tokyo, February 1965

LOVE SONG II

Si vous voulez
peignez haut dans l'air sec vos icônes de neige
entourez-les de majuscules ornées
pendant que les flocons fondent sur votre langue
alléluia!

Moi j'ai d'autres affaires
je traverse en dormant la nuit hémisphérique
derrière le velours de l'absence
je retrouve à tâtons l'amande d'un visage
soie ancienne
les yeux couchés dedans
fenêtres où je t'ai vue tant de fois accoudée
frêle et m'interrogeant
comme un signe ou comme un présage
dont on n'est pas certain d'avoir trouvé le sens

Le chant vert du loriot ne sait rien du silence.

Nord-Japon, hiver 1966

LOVE SONG II

If you wish
paint high in the dry air your snowy icons
surround them with ornate capital letters
while the flakes melt on your tongue
halleluiah!

I have other things to do
I'm sleepwalking through the hemispheric night
behind the felt of absence
and groping for the almond of a face
ancient silk
with the eyes lying in it
windows on whose sills I oft saw you leaning
frail and questioning me
as if I were a sign or an omen
whose meaning one can't be sure of having found

The oriole's green song knows nothing of silence.

North Japan, winter 1966

LOVE SONG III

Quand tisonner les mots pour un peu de couleur
ne sera plus ton affaire
quand le rouge du sorbier et la cambrure des filles
ne te feront plus regretter ta jeunesse
quand un nouveau visage tout écorné d'absence
ne fera plus trembler ce que tu croyais solide
quand le froid aura pris congé du froid
et oubli dit adieu à l'oubli
quand tout aura revêtu la silencieuse opacité du houx

ce jour-là
quelqu'un t'attendra au bord du chemin
pour te dire que c'était bien ainsi
que tu devais terminer ton voyage
démuni
tout à fait démuni

alors peut-être . . .
mais que la neige tombée cette nuit
soit aussi comme un doigt sur la bouche.

Genève, décembre 1977

LOVE SONG III

When stirring words in the fire for a little color
will no longer matter to you
when the red of the service tree and girlish curves
will no longer make you regret your youth
when a new face dog-eared with absence
will no longer shake what seemed solid
when the cold will have taken leave of the cold
and oblivion bidden farewell to oblivion
when everything will have donned the silent opaqueness of the holly

on that day
someone will wait for you at the edge of the path
to tell you it was just fine like that
that you had to end your journey
destitute
wholly destitute

perhaps, then . . .
but may the snow fallen that night
also be like a finger on your lips.

Geneva, December 1977

PIERRE CHAPPUIS

PLEINES MARGES (*extraits*)

Toute la nuit
est resté ouvert
sur une page blanche
le calepin de cuir noir.

Au matin, la neige.

(hiatus)

Neigeuse ascendance de la lumière.

Chaque pas s'allège du précédent
entré dans l'empierrement de la route.

Dans la liquide rumeur du jour
tous bruits s'annulent.

(autre matin)

Une plongée
d'ici
dans la brume.

Laineuse étendue d'eau;
lac s'élevant
dans le jour.

(heure et lieu incertains)

PIERRE CHAPPUIS

from **FULL MARGINS**

All night long
the black leather notebook
has stayed open
to a blank page.

In the morning, snow.

(hiatus)

Snowy rising of the light.

Each step casts off the previous one
that has entered the rocky roadbed.

In the daylight's liquid murmur
all noises dissolve.

(another morning)

A dive
from here
into the haze.

Wooly watery expanse;
lake rising
into daylight.

(hour and place uncertain)

D'une rue déserte l'autre
froide est, dans la main,
la rampe du ciel.

(présence de P. Reverdy)

Dans le vide, cette double note
—gabarit du brouillard—
sonne précis, sonne clair.

Insituables demeurent
—émergeront-ils?—
bord et faîte du toit.

(mésange avant midi)

Sur la page des eaux,
en vain
tu inscris ton vol.

Oiseau double
à la poursuite de toi-même.

(fugitivement)

A deserted street, another one:
cold is, in the hand,
the ramp to the sky.

(presence of P. Reverdy)

In the emptiness, this double note
—foggy outline—
sounds precise, sounds clear.

The edge and the top of the roof
—will they emerge?—
remain indefinable.

(titmouse before noon)

On the page of the waters,
in vain
you inscribe your flight.

Dual bird
chasing yourself.

(fleetingly)

JACQUES CHESSEX

LE BEAU CANAL

Me promenant le long d'un beau canal
Je songeais à La Fontaine
À ce miracle de transparence
De son poème de l'oiseau et de l'onde
À ces jours qu'il dit plus beaux que les autres jours
Et qui ont été vécus avant ma naissance
Avant la faillite et la ruine de mes instants
Alors qu'au temps de ce poète, la lumière
Était donnée une fois pour toutes
Oui jamais retirée ou salie
Et l'arbre, la pente, l'oiseau, la rivière
Épanouissaient doucement et justement leur clarté
La fine ironie et la bonté
Étaient dans l'air avec les branches et les ailes
Et sur le chemin de halage où je vais tête basse
Mon double en ce temps-là
Aurait pu s'avancer sans cette peur que j'ai
De perdre à tout instant quelque chose de l'image
Ou de son plaisir, ou du jour
Et j'eusse aussi peut-être rencontré
La perfection dans ma vie et dans mes songes écrits
À mon tour calme et heureux dans cette éternité
Où ne m'eussent pas déchiré les anges
Vengeurs de ma saison et du paysage
Pleins de souci de mon pas précaire
Jaloux de cette eau pure dans le vert

JACQUES CHESSEX

THE BEAUTIFUL CANAL

While walking along a beautiful canal
I was musing about La Fontaine
About that miracle of transparency
That is his poem about the bird and the stream
About days he says were more beautiful than other days
And that he lived through before my own birth
Before the failure and the ruin of my own moments
While in that poet's day, the light
Was granted once and for all
Yes, never withdrawn or sullied
And the tree, the slope, the bird, the stream
Would softly and justly spread their clarity
Fine irony and goodness
Were in the air with the branches and the wings
And on the towpath where I am walking with lowered head
My double back then
Could have headed forward without this fear I feel
That every instant I'm losing something of the picture
Or its pleasure or the day
And I would also have perhaps met
Perfection in my life and in my written dreams
Being in turn calm and happy in this eternity
Where the angels would not have torn me to shreds
Avengers of my season and the landscape
Carefully studying my shaky step
Jealous of this pure water in the green expanse

EN CE TEMPS-LÀ

En ce temps-là
Quand la mélancolie venait en moi
Avec l'odeur terreuse de la pluie
Où j'avais mis mon âme intrépide à l'abri de toute
                                                distraction

Quand la pluie avait lavé toute pensée inutile
Même la mélancolie
Et la tristesse était devenue aussi rare
Que le chant du tétras-lyre
Ô chant dont me souvenir avec ses tristes notes
Comme une toux de vieillard dans l'air mouillé du sombre
                                                printemps

Quand il n'y avait plus de curiosité en moi
    que celle de Dieu
Aucune autre voix dans ma tête
    que la voix des anges de Dieu
Aucun appel dans mon cœur charnel
Que celui du Seigneur rayonnant
    entre les vieux fous de l'hospice

Quand le vent chargé du souvenir des corolles
Toujours l'odeur de la pluie
Si douce que celle des cuisses de la muse
    dans la nuit ombreuse
La lune vagabonde aux cimes des monts
Les seins de la muse dans la source du glacier

Alors je te louais, Yorick, de m'avoir fait sage
Et respectueux de mon devoir de poète

IN THOSE DAYS

In those days
When melancholy would invade me
With the earthy smell of the rain
When I had sheltered my bold soul from all distractions

When the rain had washed away all useless thoughts
Even melancholy
And sadness had become as scarce
As the black grouse's song
O remember that song with its sad notes
Like an old man's cough in the humid air of the dark spring

When there was no more curiosity in me
    except about God
No other voice in my mind
    except the voices of God's angels
No calling out in my mortal heart
Except the radiant Lord's
    among the mindless men of the old people's home

When the wind full of memories of corollas
Always the smell of the rain
As sweet as the fragrant muse's thighs
    in the shadowy night
The wandering moon at the mountain peaks
The muse's breasts in the source of the glacier

Then I praised you, Yorick, to have made me wise
And respectful of my poet's duty
I loved you for having bequeathed me ruins
And the voluptuous song of this rubble

Je t'aimais de m'avoir donné la ruine en partage
Et le chant voluptueux de ces décombres
Pour faire mieux mon travail parmi ces ombres
À ton exemple associant le rire et son contraire
Au fil des heures mêlant mes règnes
Le goût plus fort de la journée et le miel des morts

So I can better do my work among these shadows
Imitating you by joining laughter to its opposite
As the hours go by mixing my reigns
The stronger taste of the day and the honey of the dead

PIERRE-ALAIN TÂCHE

MATIN D'OCTOBRE À CHAVORNAY

Ce fut un matin d'espace intact et juste,
comme la jeune colère du dieu ancien,
un matin ajusté aux halliers, peignant
la laine de brume écrue, resserrée au vallon
où la mort en rond rôde à la trace des chiens.

Ce fut un deuil d'épine noire
sur l'iris innombrable et sourd,
qui fait la vie profonde, ouverte,
et nos mains lourdes de prunelles.

Tout un matin, je n'ai voulu nul autre lieu
que cet angle de bois touffu, portant
sur un pré courbe où l'herbe monte,
où le pas dresse la rosée et scintille.

Ici se tient la proie que je désire.

Un règne est dans les branches du silence
—et le vent laboure, et le froid
rend la retraite étroite et difficile.

PIERRE-ALAIN TÂCHE

OCTOBER MORNING IN CHAVORNAY

It was a morning when space was just, intact,
like the ancient god's youthful anger,
a morning befitting thickets, carding
the raw woolly haze held tightly in the small valley
where death roams around following hunting dogs.

It was a bereavement of blackthorn
over the countless deaf irises of eyes,
which deepens and opens up life,
and lades our hands with sloes.

For one entire morning I wanted no other place
than this corner of a dense woods looking down
on a curved meadow with rising grass,
where each step pricks up the dew and glistens.

Here hides the prey I desire.

A reign lies in the branches of silence
—and the wind plows on, and the cold
makes retreat narrow and difficult.

Soudain, comme aux grands jours d'hiver,
la neige, la terre où fuira le retour.
Soudain, la vertigineuse tendresse du retour,
les épis de mémoire enfouis sous les labours,
l'enfance aux murs des vignes de vin court,
l'heureuse nudité dans le jardin premier
où riait la cousine au ventre bien fendu,
et cette course avide comme on rêve
jusqu'à la cuisine chaude où la Mère
pose un baiser frais sur le front.

LE LOINTAIN OPÉRA

Un rideau de fer est tombé, vers le soir.
Au-dessus de l'eau noire, un fabuleux décor
entre, très lentement, dans le port,
et s'illumine, et veut chanter.

Othello court, sous les arcades de la nuit.
L'errance de ses mains ne trompe pas,
si sa voix ne vient pas encore jusques à nous.
Les bois n'ont pas perdu racines et les vents,
sans lieu, peuplent la treille éparse sur nos fronts.
L'ouverture est attente et suspens.
Chaque air, en nous, préserve sa fraîcheur.

Suddenly, as in the great days of winter,
the snow, the soil into which its return will flee.
Suddenly, the dizzying tenderness of this return,
memory's ears of wheat plowed under the soil,
childhood on the walls of the vineyard with its acidic wine,
the blissful nudity in the primordial garden
where the girl cousin with her wide slit would laugh,
and this running as desirous as dreaming
all the way to the warm kitchen where the Mother
plants a fresh kiss on the forehead.

THE DISTANT OPERA

An iron curtain has fallen, toward evening.
Above the black water, fabulous scenery
slowly slips into the harbor
and lights up, and wants to sing.

Othello runs beneath the arches of the night.
His roaming hands fool no one,
even if his voice has not reached us.
The woods still have roots and the homeless winds
people the scattered vine arbor on our foreheads.
The overture is expectation and in suspense.
Every aria, in us, keeps its freshness.

Et quand je m'en reviens, je vois
la volière de nos enfants habiles à jeter,
sans vraiment se pencher au-dehors,
des bulles ou des astres irisés,
promis aux galaxies des remblais sans fin

—mots ou messages que l'on sème,
au hasard, sur l'archipel des poussiers,
qui fit si longuement barrage à notre élan,
quand nous allions vers la piazza,
couvant un maigre feu sous la langue.

BALTHUS MONTAGNARD

L'adolescente au regard sans limite,
aux cernes de cristal, au front bombé,
dit ne plus supporter le jour;
elle court soudain vers la chambre d'arolle,
elle s'affale, elle s'endort et son lit
devient torrent de braises, sous le vent,
quand elle désire ou rêve ou s'abandonne
à l'avalanche que la frondaison
laisse glisser sous la clameur d'été,
sans autre attente que la mer.

And when I come back home, I see
the aviary of our children skilled at blowing out,
without really leaning outside,
bubbles or iridescent stars,
promised to galaxies of endless embankments

—randomly sown words or messages
on the coal-dust archipelago
that blocked our élan for so long
when we were heading toward the piazza,
nurturing a weak fire below the tongue.

BALTHUS THE MOUNTAIN MAN

The adolescent girl with her boundless gaze,
crystal rings below her eyes, her forehead domed,
says she no longer stands the daylight;
suddenly she streaks toward the arolla-paneled room,
collapses, falls asleep, and her bed
becomes a torrent of embers in the wind,
when she desires or dreams or gives herself up
to the avalanche that the foliage
lets slip beneath the summery clamor,
with no other expectation than the sea.

PIERRE VOÉLIN

DANS UNE PRAIRIE DE FAUCHE (*extraits*)

Dans ma bouche les mots deviennent pénombre
et myosotis—syllabes de tendre lumière
pour celle que troublera le cœur

Viendras-tu saison brusquer les eaux froides
arracher leurs ailes aux petits faucons
ou séparer mes lèvres de leur sang

*

Sous l'écorce et la feuille mince du bouleau
silence tu t'abrites—et je m'abrite

Et toi pareille à la rose de l'ange de Silésie
belle tu es belle d'être sans pourquoi

Même les ombres aujourd'hui sont propices

Le blé va surgir et poser l'été sur des tiges
pour toi qui doutes et marches haletante
vers ton commencement

PIERRE VOÉLIN

from IN A HAY MEADOW

In my mouth words become penumbra
and forget-me-nots—syllables of tender light
for she whom the heart will disturb

Season, will you come and hasten the cold waters
tear the wings off baby falcons
or separate my lips from their blood

    *

Below the bark and the thin leaf of the birch
you take shelter, silence—and I take shelter

And you are equal to the Silesian Angel's rose
beautiful you are, beautiful in being without whys

Even the shadows today are favorable

The wheat will surge forth and place summer on stems
for you who doubt and walk panting
toward your beginning

Bûchers du silence—l'amour s'y découvre
instants éclats branches aux églantines
que brûle la terre d'été

Brûlent tes lèvres mes doigts qui les touchent
les saisons trop lentes où vont les rapaces
brille le nom tremblé le nom secret

fleur hier épiée entre les pas de l'eau

*

Paroles qui volent pour toi lointaines
qui nagent à la proue des étoiles
voyageuses aimées par le feu

paroles ce jour
qui reviennent effleurer mes lèvres
avec les herbes plus frêles sous le vent
les ombres lentes que peignent les roseaux

Pyres of silence—love stands revealed
moments sparkles branches of wild rose
burned by the summer soil

Your burning lips my fingers touching them
the too slow seasons to which fly birds of prey
the tremulous name the secret name shines

flower spotted yesterday between the steps of the water

    *

Faraway words flying for you
swimming at the prow of the stars
fire-beloved travelers

words this day
coming back to graze my lips
with the grasses grown frailer in the wind
the slow shadows combed by the reeds

Et je l'ai su—alors tu me suivrais
toi la plus lointaine et proche
comme une étoile vagabonde
avec ses rires brodés
lumière à jamais
lumière parjure
serment de hauts feuillages
dans la transparence du cœur

*

Vite entrez dans la table des constellations
belettes feuillages et vous chevreuils

La boue fait voler ses sabots à mon visage
Et mes yeux se murent lentement

Que s'en aillent les faucons
Qu'ils jettent leurs cris aux citernes

Que s'accomplisse la douleur

And I knew it—so you would follow me
you the farthest and the nearest
like a roving star
with its embroidered laughs
ever a light
a betraying light
an oath of tall foliage
in the transparent heart

       *

Weasels leaves and you roebucks
quick enter the constellation table

The mud makes its hooves fly up to my face
And my eyes slowly wall themselves up

May the falcons fly away
May they toss their cries into the cisterns

May pain now be accomplished

POÈMES DE NOVEMBRE

Jean-Christophe Æby, in memoriam

N'oubliez pas la poésie
ni le poème qui dort
comme un enfant dans la mémoire

S'il n'appelait plus la nuit
dans le tourment d'un mauvais songe?

Bâillonné? simplement farouche
attendant qu'on se taise,
patiemment, au coin du bois

*

Quand retrouverai-je le temps d'écrire?

Les gens partiront sans moi qui resterai là
parmi les feuilles, près du tilleul

n'ayant plus qu'à sentir le temps
presque sans bouger passer comme
la lumière entre les branches

*

Je ne sais quelle est cette voix
ni ce qui parle quand il fait noir

FRÉDÉRIC WANDELÈRE

NOVEMBER POEMS

Jean-Christophe Aeby: in memoriam

Don't forget poetry
nor the poem sleeping
like a child in memory

What if it no longer beckoned to the night,
tormented by a bad dream?

Gagged? simply shy, unshakeable,
patiently waiting for everyone
to stop speaking in the corner of the woods

*

When will I find the time to write?

Everyone will leave without me, I'll linger
among the leaves near the lime tree,

needing only to sense time,
almost without moving, passing
like light between the branches

*

I don't know what that voice is,
nor what speaks when it is dark

—La musique à peine entendue, cette rumeur
qui se couche avec moi, me tenant en éveil

me guidant de bruit en bruit
comme un aveugle mais sûr . . .

Qui saurait aller sans douter
parmi les odeurs et les bruits?

      *

Si ma vie est trop pauvre
pour que le chant s'y arrête
comme la graine sous les feuilles
qui dure patiemment tout l'hiver,

ou trop laide pour qu'une mélodie
s'y dessine encore, qui m'en voudra?

Même le moineau reviendrait à ma fenêtre
comme si la musique s'y tenait toujours,
s'y faisait toute seule entendre
—et mieux encore en mon absence!

      *

Est-ce le poème qui me tourmente
ou moi qui le cherche sans le trouver?

Au fond des yeux, léger, peu l'épouvante
qui sait se taire ou se donner

—The music barely heard, a murmur
that lies down with me, keeping me awake

guiding me from noise to noise
like a blind man but sure . . .

Who can walk without doubts
among the smells and the noises?

*

If my life is too poor
for song to make a halt there
like a seed beneath leaves
patiently lasting out the winter,

or too ugly for a melody
to form there again, who will hold it against me?

Even the sparrow would come back to my window
as if music still cared about being there,
could be heard there all by itself
—and even better in my absence!

*

Is it the poem that torments me
or me seeking it without success?

Lightweight, deep in the eyes, little matter the dread
that can stop speaking or give itself over

FRANÇOIS DEBLUË

PATIENCE D'UN ÉCLAIR

Longtemps prémédité
si vif
si fuyant pourtant
de ses grands réseaux
l'éclair illumine
le ciel   la terre
toute la nuit du monde

Et longtemps
sa trace demeure
à l'œil de l'homme apeuré.

PATIENCE D'UN HOMME ASSOIFFÉ

D'une main tremblante
porte le verre à ses lèvres
boit
malgré serments et promesses
boit
ses grands yeux étonnés
d'enfant à la nuit livré
il boit
appelle   (mais qui l'entendra?)
ne sait
faire taire autrement
cette peur à son ventre
la mort devant lui

FRANÇOIS DEBLUË

PATIENCE OF A FLASH OF LIGHTNING

Long premeditated
so quick
yet so fleeting
with its great network
the lightning brightens
the sky   the earth
all the world's night

And long its trace
lingers
in the fearful man's eye.

PATIENCE OF A THIRSTY MAN

With a shaky hand
brings the glass to his lips
drinks
despite pledges promises
drinks
his big astonished eyes
of a child handed over to the night
he drinks
calls out   (but who will hear him?)
not knowing otherwise
how to silence
this fear in his gut
death facing him

boit
le vin au fond de son verre
le verre renversé à ses lèvres
tout son sang mêlé de tous les alcools
usures et rasades
appelle:

qu'on lui accorde au moins
l'apaisement d'une ultime brûlure.

PASSION DE L'HOMME BAFOUÉ

Sur lui ne cessent de crier
leur rage   leur colère
à sa face crachant
injures et malédictions
leur haine sans fin
leur injuste passion

S'il n'est dieu fait homme
comment
saisi d'effroi
comment ne tremblerait-il pas?

S'il n'est ange souverain
quel frein à son malheur
—à toutes les tourmentes en lui?

drinks
down to the dregs in his glass
the glass tipped back to his lips
his blood blended with all the liquors
worn out & bottoms up
he calls out:

may he be granted at least
the appeasement of an ultimate burn.

PASSION OF THE SCORNED MAN

At him keep shouting
their rage   their anger
at his face keep spitting
insults curses
their endless hate
their unjust passion

If he is not god made man
how then
overcome by fear
would he not tremble?

If he's not a sovereign angel
what curb on his unhappiness
—on all his inner torments?

PATIENCE DE L'HOMME MENDIANT

De soif et de détresse
ce corps (le sien à peine)
tremble et tremble encore

Toutes espérances perdues
regard absent   bras engourdi
    il attend
d'un inconnu   d'un passant
    il attend
l'improbable
l'impossible amour.

PATIENCE OF THE BEGGAR

Out of thirst and distress
that body (barely his own)
trembles and keeps trembling

All hope lost
empty gaze   numbed arm
    he expects
from a stranger   from a passerby
    he expects
an improbable
an impossible love.

JOSÉ-FLORE TAPPY

LUNAIRES (*extraits*)

Accroupis
les enfants eux aussi
fouillent la terre

Entre roues et bidons
ils échangent leurs affaires
éclats de verre couvercles
menue monnaie
parfois dans les décharges
mettent la main
sur une vipère

c'est leur peau tiède
leur peau trop brune
que le serpent convoite

      *

La nuit venue
une fois couverts
d'un fin brouillard
couchés sur la terre froide
c'est la lune qui les berce

de son crachin
elle dépoussière
leurs chevelures de paille

      *

JOSÉ-FLORE TAPPY

from LUNAR POEMS

Squatting
the children also
rummage the ground

Amid wheels and cans
they swap things
lids bits of glass
small change
sometimes in the dumps
they put their hands
on a viper

it's their lukewarm skin
their overly brown skin
that the snake covets

                *

At nightfall
once thin fog
covers them
lying on the cold ground
the moon cradles them

with its drizzle
washes the dust off
their strawlike hair

                *

Soluble
elle a fondu
la lune
dans la cuvette
s'est mélangée
comme un savon
à l'eau glacée
elle éclaire le fer blanc

Saura-t-elle guérir l'âcreté
fermer les gerçures
réparer la fatigue

peut-être

Plonger nos mains nos bras
dans cette huile
ces paillettes

*

Cage de buée
suspendue à quel clou
quelle étoile sombre

Elle ballotte elle oscille
dans la nuit pauvre
la nuit fertile

lanterne pour les marins
les oubliés les égarés

*

The soluble
moon
has melted
in the big bowl
has blended
like a bar of soap
into the icy water
shines on the tin

Will it heal the acridity
close up the cracked lips
repair the weariness

perhaps

To sink our hands our arms
into this oil
these sequins

*

Cage of mist
hanging from what nail
what dark star

it swings bobs about
in the barren night
the fertile night

a lantern for sailors
the lost the forgotten

*

Mais la lune vers la terre
parfois se tourne
de quel rivage
vient-elle
hublot de quel navire
de quel paquebot
à la dérive

On voudrait l'approcher
tendre vers elle un doigt
oser seulement
pousser sa vitre opaque

*

Entre île et continent
sous la dalle mouvante
des vagues
un jour reposeront
toutes nos vies mêlées

invisibles
seul le vent tournera
sur nos voix disparues

But the moon sometimes turns
toward the earth
from what shore
does it come
of what ship
what drifting ocean liner
is it the porthole

You would like to draw near
to reach out your finger
just daring to push
its opaque windowpane

                    *

Between island and continent
beneath the moving slab
of the waves
one day will lie
invisibly

all our mingled lives
only the wind will revolve
around our vanished voices

Quand la nuit déploiera
ses grandes ailes de granit
quand les maisons rouleront
comme du gravier
dans un ciel distendu
en douce
je m'en irai

toutes mes affaires
dans la brouette du vent
partirai
partirai loin

When the night unfurls
its big granite wings
when the houses roll
like gravel
in a distended sky
on the quiet
I will slip away

all my belongings
in the wheelbarrow of the wind
I will go away
go far away

SYLVIANE DUPUIS

EMBLÈMES (*extraits*)

TOMBES

Les esprits remuants
qu'on enterre à l'écart,
que sait-on de leurs jeux
dans le dos des vivants?

La lisière d'arbres, à l'orée des villes,
ce n'est pas le désert qu'elle barre
—mais l'inquiétant loisir
des trépassés
qui marmonnent sous le bâillon
si peu pesant
du sable.

                *   *
                   *

On rencontre d'abord
les enfants
et les morts:
ceux qui ont en commun
le berceau, le savoir
et l'opaque mutisme.

SYLVIANE DUPUIS

from EMBLEMS

GRAVES

Restless spirits buried
just outside of town:
who knows what games they play
behind the backs of the living?

When they border city limits,
trees keep back not the desert
but rather the disturbing leisure
of the dead
mumbling away beneath
the nearly weightless
gag of the sand.

      *   *
        *

First you meet
the children
and the dead:
those who share
the cradle, knowledge
and opaque silence.

MORTS PRÉMATURÉMENT

Pauvres morts, qu'on oublie
sans corps, dans l'inachevé
—ô impuissants
dormeurs
sous le signe de pierre,
dont l'âme qui hésite
tour à tour entre
et sort:

qu'une odeur noire émeuve
la narine d'un dieu,
et que soient délivrés
vos souffles qui divaguent
aux quatre directions!

* *
*

Parfois, si la terre tremble
on voit jaillir des niches
ces bouddhas oubliés
dans les murs
qui rient sous le séisme,
imperturbablement.

UNTIMELY DEATHS

Poor dead people, whom we forget
are bodiless, amid incompleteness
—O powerless
sleepers,
beneath the stone signs,
whose hesitating souls
in turn go out,
come back in:

may a black stench move
a god's nostril
so your breaths wandering
in all four directions
will be freed!

              *   *
                 *

Sometimes, when the ground shakes
those buddhas forgotten
in walls
spring from their niches and laugh
during the earthquake
imperturbably.

CLAIRE GENOUX

HIVER

Cet hiver plaqué à la rive des arbres
ces matins où le soleil n'éclaire plus
tout ce qui se précipitera contre le mur des lèvres
—les gravats le bois des grandes portes
on devra le retenir à l'aveugle
mais quelque part au bas des jardins cousus de saules
on nous aura laissé
—ballotté par le vent
notre mince poumon d'herbe

ÉTRANGLEMENT

Quelque chose en moi résiste et s'étrangle
inflammable au moindre souffle
à quoi bon y revenir
ce qu'à moi-même je n'ose confier
—silence contre silence
mon oreille collée aux murs des granges l'entend
et sur ce fil
va ma vie

CLAIRE GENOUX

WINTER

This winter plastered against the banks of trees
these mornings when the sun doesn't shine anymore
everything that will smash into the wall of lips
—the rubble the wood of great doors
one should blindly hold on to it all
but somewhere at the bottom of gardens sewn with willows
will have been left behind for us
—beaten by the wind—
our thin lung of grass.

CHOKING

Something in me resists and chokes
blazes up at the slightest breath
what's the use going back to it
what I dare not confide to myself
—silence against silence
my ear pressed against barn walls hears it
and my life runs
along this thread

II
ITALIAN

TRANSLATED BY
SIMON KNIGHT (SK) AND
JAMIE RICHARDS (JR)

FRANCESCO CHIESA

FUOCHI DI PRIMAVERA

O allegre crepitanti, sull'orlo de' prati, vermiglie
fiamme, nel tempo argenteo, fuochi di primavera!

S'abbruciano le morte, le inutili cose oggi: quante
son foglie che non tornano più verdi, bucce vuote;

i pruni che non hanno più pungoli, appesi al ciliegio
già tutt'in fiore; i salici stanchi di più legare . . .

Sparano brevi irosi i ciottoli nella profonda
brace; la fiamma, un attimo rotta, più fiera rugge.

Pallide celestine volute di fumo dall'ampia
campagna, fra le lucide selve, nell'aria molle,

levansi; e sciami sciami di brune falene . . . In un' acre
fragranza si confondono cenere e violette.

Fiato di violette di sotto il concio arido sorge;
puntano con i teneri capi i narcisi a uscire.

Verde fra l'erbe gialle la nuova erba brulica. I crochi
su guizzano. Le primule sciolgono gli occhi d'oro . . .

Via, tristi cose! Armate d'un grande lor pettine manda
all'opera ogni casa oggi le sue fanciulle.

Cinte le tempie d'una vermiglia pezzuola, le gaie
rimondatrici, il rapido pettine menan entro

FRANCESCO CHIESA

SPRING BONFIRES

Oh cheerful crackling flames, spring bonfires,
deep red in the silvery light on the meadows' edge!

The dead, the useless things are being burned today:
leaves that will not again turn green, empty husks;

thornless brambles, hanging on the cherry-tree
already in full bloom; osiers tired of being tied . . .

Stones deep in the embers angry split and spit;
the flame dies down, then fiercer still ascends.

Pale light-blue wreaths of smoke rise in the soft air
mid fresh-faced woods from open countryside;

and swarms, swarms of flakes of brownish ash . . .
In acrid fragrance ash and violets mix.

Breath of violets transpires from 'neath the dry manure;
up spring the tender heads of 'mergent daffodils.

Green 'midst the yellowed tufts, the fresh grass seethes.
Crocuses spurt forth. Cowslips loose their golden cups . . .

Away, sad things! Armed with broad rakes
each household sets its girls to work today.

Foreheads bound in bright red scarves,
the merry clearers deploy deft rakes among

gl'ispidi velli, i tetri fogliami, le stipule, i ricci.
S'innalza sulle stridule lische il lor canto nuovo.

E il mio . . . —Via, vecchie foglie! Passato è il vostro
anno. Ed un altro
comincia. I rami mettono lustre le nuove gemme . . .

Cantano. E il mucchio cresce crosciante. E celeste dal mucchio
snodasi il fumo. Rosea balza la fiamma a volo.

"SOLE DI PRIMAVERA . . ."

Sole di primavera, io non sapevo
che sí bello tu fossi e grande e nuovo,

né tal dolcezza se le mani muovo
nel tuo lume dorato e di te bevo.

Veder cose, udir voci è tal sollievo
che di chiudere ancor gli occhi mi provo
per il piacer di riaprirli; e trovo
la perduta mia voce e un grido levo.

E anche gli alberi, i monti, l'erbe . . . Un volto
di meraviglia oggi la terra, fisso
nella celeste fiamma onde si pasce.

E anch'io . . . Guardo il sol giovane che nasce;
guardo fin alla cecità l'abisso
donde egli sorge, il rombo d'oro ascolto.

the tangled layers, dull leaf litter, stubble, chestnut casings.
Above the piercing chatter arises their new song.

And mine . . . Away, old leaves. Your year is
done. And another
begins. The branches put out bright new buds . . .

They sing. The roaring bonfire grows. Sky-blue from the heap
the smoke curls up. And rose-red leaps the flame into the air.

"SPRINGTIME SUN . . ."

Springtime sun, I hadn't a clue
so handsome you were and big and new,

nor so gentle if my hands I move
in your golden light and drink of you.

To see things, hear voices is such relief,
I find my lost voice and banish my grief.
And once more my eyes up tight I screw
for the pleasure of opening them anew.

And also the trees, the mountains, the grass . . .
Gazing rapt on the flame in which it basks,
There is wonder today on the face of the earth.

And I too . . . I watch the sun in its birth,
blindly watch the abyss where it rises so bold
and hear in my ears the thunder of gold.

SK

VALERIO ABBONDIO

PAROLE

Povera voce mia, che esiti e tremi,
quando ti sforzo a dire quel che vedo
perfetto e saldo, perché unito sempre
all'arcana virtù dell'universo.
E se parole ripeti che ascolto
interne, falsa suoni, o troppo forte:
tu che tenti d'esprimer i silenzi.

SPIRITO

Grandeggia il monte verso il cielo: meno
di un punto sulla Terra: anch'essa un'ombra
minima in seno all'universo: e Tu,
Spirito, tutto in Te contieni e avvivi,
fuor d'ogni spazio e tempo, onnipresente.
D'intender come sia, invano cerco:
guardo il sereno purissimo, e adoro.

QUELLA FIUMANA

Quella fiumana pallida attraverso
il firmamento: donde viene, dove
va? Sulle sponde le costellazioni
scintillano: tu miri, fonda e lieve,
la remota riviera di silenzio.

VALERIO ABBONDIO

WORDS

My poor voice, you falter and tremble
when I push you to say what I see as
perfect and solid, what is always united
with the arcane virtue of the universe.
And if you repeat words that I hear
inside, you sound false, or too loud:
you who try to express the silences.

SPIRIT

The peak towers toward the sky, less
than a speck on the Earth, it too a minor
shadow in the bosom of the universe: and You,
Spirit, contain and enliven all within Yourself,
outside all space and time, omnipresent.
To understand how this could be, in vain I try:
In worship, I watch the flawless sky.

THAT STREAM

That pale stream surging through
the firmament: whence does it come, where
does it go? At its shores the constellations
shimmer: you observe it, deep and light,
the remote riviera of silence.

IL MONDO TI SI SVELA

Il mondo ti si svela in verità
più che in bellezza; e un po' ti attristi, e pensi
un tempo non lontano in cui bastava
un colore, un accordo, a darti un senso
superno. Più a fondo ora la mente
guarda le cose e la virtù che insieme
le rinnova; e pur godi, se intravedi
bellezza e verità come un sol volto.

THE WORLD IS REVEALED TO YOU

The world reveals itself more in truth
than in beauty; and you get a bit sad, and think
of a time not so long ago when all it took
was a color, a harmony, to give you a sense
of the celestial. Now the mind looks at things
more deeply and virtue that makes them
new, together; and it satisfies you, to glimpse
truth and beauty as one face.

JR

GIOVANNI BIANCONI

FINAL

Contrabass da la mort
la cassa ca squariga giü in la tomba
e ca crica süi cord;
quàtar manad da tera ca rimbomba
sül vöid dal querc; bocch storgiud dai sangiott
strozzaa dent in la gora;
öcc tórbor dal gran piang
e lì fiss sü la bara
ca scompariss sott tera: bastiment
ca sa sprofonda dent in l'aqua mara.

RICÒVAR

Pori vegitt setaa
sü la bancheta al soo, la schena al mür,
cavii gris, vestii scür,
facett patid, con quii öcc stracch e bon
ca varda al via vai
dal stradon e di tren ca passa via,
pori vecc stracch e smort
a m' parii di vagon
ca specia fermi süi binari mort.

GIOVANNI BIANCONI

FINALE

Double bass of death
the case slides down in the ground
creaking on the strings beneath;
four handfuls of dirt resound
on the hollow lid; mouths twisted with sobs
stifled in the throat;
eyes flooded with tears low
and glued there to the casket
vanishing into the earth: cargo
into bitter waters set.

REST HOME

Poor little old folks sitting
on a bench in the sun, backs to the wall,
gray hair, dark clothes,
pale faced, with their kind tired eyes
watching the hustle and bustle
of the main road and the passing trains,
poor old folks waxen and slack
look to me like train cars waiting
motionless on dead tracks.

AL SCIOR CÜRAD FÖRA DI STRASC

Mei i zìnzan i zòcor i zibrett
al cröcch di pee i cavii dispecenaa
e chell'odor caldüsc d'impissoldaa
di picch—bonora—e di pori vegett,

che gnanca—dopo—tücc chii mezz calzett
a la messa di des: bisg pitüraa:
e, pesg che pesg, chell'eterno rivaa
a mezz vangeli da la sciora Ziett.

La s'strüscia dent, tüta belee e anei,
scolada profümada in gran toalett,
tramezz di óman e di ganivei

in pee in fond a la gesa: e vöi scomett
che, pa 'l rest da la messa, i men porscei
i penserà domà a ciapp e a tett . . .

THE PARISH PRIEST LOSES HIS WITS

Better the clogs the scuffs the rags
the dirty feet and hair a mess
and that warmish scent of piss
of the farmers—first thing—and little old hags,

even worse—later—all those second-raters,
painted and polished, at the ten o'clock Mass
and worst of all, the arrival, endless,
halfway through the Gospel: Signora Lucietta's.

She files in, all trinkets and rings,
dress low cut, perfumed, all done up,
surrounded by the men and boys standing

at the back of the church: and I'd cast my bets
for the rest of the Mass, even the last to lust
are thinking of nothing but backsides and breasts . . .

JR

GIUSEPPE ZOPPI

LA COLLINA

Nel mattino d'autunno la collina
brillava al sole: argentea di brina.

Oltre il suo arco, amoroso si apriva
il cielo della mia terra nativa.

A mezza costa un umile ciliegio
aveva ancora un suo tardivo fregio

di foglie, rosse come il nuovo vino . . .
E dall'ispido intrico d'uno spino,

s'alzava al cielo un'esile betulla
candida come un braccio di fanciulla.

GIUSEPPE ZOPPI

THE HILL

In the autumn morning the frosted hill
shone in the sunlight, silver and chill.

Beyond its arch, the amorous sky
opened its arms to draw me nigh.

A humble cherry on the slope half way
still bore a late and lingering spray

of wine-red leaves from the tree not torn . . .
And from a patch of bramble thorn

a birch tree reached for the deep blue calm
white and slim as a maiden's arm.

                                                                SK

PINO BERNASCONI

BISSA RÓSSA BIZERESCA

Bissa róssa bizeresca
internada là in di Sciss,
e biss celèst, in tund,
che fann cuncèrt: incant
che grema l'öcc al catabiss,
stralüsc che svia la becada
di falchitt. Bissa dal magg,
lüsenta al mèl
di pegurèll in cumpra
che in la taneta sentan
i barinöö che pican.
Bissa dal fard,
sül lungh di ruertiis,
al zard da zev dre la veleta alzada.

LA SIRA DI ANIM

Viagia, stassira, d'alp in alp, la prima
filèra di anim
che lassan la Tèra.

Sa ferman ai varch. A pizzan i ciar
par quii divagan
a scriv i salüd sü la scòrza
di láras. Sa tócan,
sa parlan, sa prövan i al
in dal ciel di litani. Vann via.

PINO BERNASCONI

RED CRESTED BASILISK

Red crested basilisk,
hiding up on the Sciss,
and cerulean snakes, encircled,
in concert: casting a spell
that scorches the snake-catcher's eye,
a flash that deflects the peck
of the kestrel. Snake of spring,
glistening round the ruff
of the sheep heavy with pup
who can feel the lambs
in their bellies kicking.
Snake of the rouge,
along the edge of the hops,
the slick risk behind the raised veil.

NIGHT OF SOULS

Tonight, in transit, from peak
to peak, the first line of souls
leaving the Earth.

Pausing at each pass, they light candles
for the travelers to write
their good-byes on the bark
of the larch trees. Touching,
talking, trying out their wings
in the sky of litanies. They depart.

JR

FELICE MENGHINI

PAESAGGIO GRIGIO

È una timida primavera
che sorride attraverso l'aria grigia
indistinto viso
d'una bellezza forse femminile
che appare dietro il vetro
di uno specchio appannato.

Anche il bruno delle sponde
si confonde
con il grigio tremolare dell'acque
nel lago silenzioso
e svaniscono i tetti rossi
col fumo quasi invisibile
dei loro camini
in un cielo ch'è simile al lago.

Dolce paesaggio veduto
in un giorno di speranze
come un occhio velato lo vedrebbe
fra qualche lacrima
che già lascia indovinare
il fiore aperto
di un vicino sorriso.

FELICE MENGHINI

GRAY LANDSCAPE

It's a timid spring
through the gray air smiling
an indistinct face
of a perhaps feminine beauty
appearing behind the surface
of a misted-up mirror.

And the duskiness of the shores
is indistinct
from the gray trembling waters
of the lake, silent
and the red rooftops vanish
with the near-invisible smoke
billowing from chimneys
into a sky that's like the lake.

A soft landscape seen
on a day of hopes
as a veiled eye would see
through certain tears
that offer a glimpse
of the open flower
of an imminent smile.

JR

ADOLFO JENNI

RAGAZZA DI PAESE

Scende la sera calma sul tuo orto,
ragazza di paese. E tu alla fine,
dopo avere nel giorno coltivato
le sue aiuole diritte, con soltanto
una striscia di fiori (astri e mammole),
ti siedi sulla panca, ti riposi.
Fai sogni da ragazza e hai speranze
ordinate: l'amore, casa e orto.
Intanto gli occhi penetranti guardano
il mobile teatro di chi passa
di là dal tuo recinto: poche e note
persone per la via ormai azzurra;
e, brava come sei, formi opinioni
sul loro aspetto e ricordi i caratteri.

Ma un giorno passerà uno dei giovani.
Ti piacerà e sbaglierai giudizio.
Un istante, e il tuo corso diversifica.
Unirai la tua vita a quella sua
dispettosa e infingarda. Sarai tu
a portarne la pena, coi tuoi figli.
Resisterai, decisa e attiva, guida
a lui stesso. Cosí trascorsi gli anni
e anziana di paese, magra, dura,
avrai consolazione unica a sera
il riposo da sola sulla verde
panca, dell'orto sempre tua fatica,
senza la fascia più dei fiori miti.

ADOLFO JENNI

VILLAGE GIRL

Dusk descends calm on your garden,
village girl. And at last,
having spent the day cultivating
the carefully aligned beds, with just
one strip of flowers (asters and violets),
you sit on the bench and take your rest.
You dream a girl's dreams,
straightforward hopes: love, home, and garden.
Meanwhile your sharp eyes watch
the shifting drama of those passing
beyond your enclosure: the few, well-known
faces on the road now in shadow;
and, in your tidy way, you form opinions
of their looks and call to mind their characters.

But one day one of the young men will pass.
You'll fall for him, careless in your judgment.
A moment, and your world changes course.
You will join your life to his,
shiftless and mean-hearted. It will be you
who bears the burden, you and your children.
You will endure, active and determined, guide
and leader. So, many years later,
become a village elder, wasted, bony,
your only consolation of an evening
will be to rest alone on the green
bench, the garden still yours to toil in,
but without the strip of gentle flowers.

Non più al futuro, penserai al passato.
Con nostalgia della ragazza ch'eri,
libera e quieta e, davanti, ogni scelta.

No longer to the future, but to the past your thoughts will go.
With nostalgia for the girl you were,
free and untroubled, with all of life before you.

SK

GIORGIO ORELLI

SERA A BEDRETTO

Salva la Dama asciutta. Viene il Matto.
Gridano i giocatori di tarocchi.
Dalle mani che pesano
cade avido il Mondo,
scivola innocua la Morte.

Le capre, giunte quasi sulla soglia
dell'osteria,
si guardano lunatiche e pietose
negli occhi,
si provano la fronte
con urti sordi.

L'ORA ESATTA

In quest'alba che quasi non odora
di fieno e di letame
i padroni di tutto il Viale
della Stazione sono tre piccioni
partiti insieme da presso l'ardita
bottega ove si vende
l'orologio che segna
L'ORA ESATTA PER TUTTA LA VITA.

GIORGIO ORELLI

EVENING IN BEDRETTO

The lone Queen is safe. Here comes the Fool.
The tarot players yell.
From their heavy hands
the World falls avid,
Death slips innocuous.

The goats, almost at the threshold
of the osteria,
inspect each other, crazed and piteous
in the eyes,
they butt heads
with dull blows.

THE EXACT TIME

In this dawn with almost no odor
of hay or manure
the masters of the entire Viale
della Stazione are three pigeons
together departed from the brave
boutique where they sell
the watch that keeps
THE EXACT TIME FOR LIFE.

NEL CERCHIO FAMILIARE

Una luce funerea, spenta,
raggela le conifere
dalla scorza che dura oltre la morte,
e tutto è fermo in questa conca
scavata con dolcezza dal tempo:
nel cerchio familiare
da cui non ha senso scampare.

Entro un silenzio così conosciuto
i morti sono più vivi dei vivi:
da linde camere odorose di canfora
scendono per le botole in stufe
rivestite di legno, aggiustano i propri ritratti,
tornano nella stalla a rivedere i capi
di pura razza bruna.

                    Ma,
senza ferri da talpe, senza ombrelli
per impigliarvi rondini;
non cauti, non dimentichi in rincorse,
dietro quale carillon ve ne andate,
ragazzi per i prati intirizziti?

La cote è nel suo corno.
Il pollaio s'appoggia al suo sambuco.
I falangi stanno a lungo intricati
sui muri della chiesa.
La fontana con l'acqua si tiene compagnia.
Ed io, restituito
a un più discreto amore della vita . . .

IN THE FAMILY CIRCLE

A funereal light, faint,
chills the firs with their
bark that outlasts death
and all is still in this valley
by time hollowed out softly:
in the family circle
there's no sense in escape.

Amid such a familiar silence
the dead live more than the living:
they come down from clean camphor-
scented rooms, through the hatches into
wood-lined *Stuben*, straighten their own
portraits, head to the stables to check on
the purebred brown cows.

                    But—
with nothing to hunt moles, no umbrellas
to catch swallows;
careless, oblivious in your capers,
what *carillon* are you running after,
boys, through the frozen fields?

The whetstone is in its horn.
The henhouse rests against its elder.
Harvestmen linger entangled
across the walls of the church.
The water keeps the fountain company.
And me, restored
to a more modest love of life . . .

LETTERA DA BELLINZONA

Una fascina d'anni, una collina.
E il castello più alto.
Tutto il grigio all'altezza dei colombi,
tutto il verde che scorre fino al grigio . . .
Ma oggi, senza desiderio, avendoti
come un'icona dentro il portafogli,
con incredibile piacere seguo
la verde traiettoria d'una stella filante,
scoccata dalla mano d'un ragazzo
fermo a metà dell'albero
della cuccagna, pago
di starsene così. L'aria rosata
che si raccoglie nella sua camicia,
il vespro a poco a poco
l'ha versata su tutta la collina.
Grida un tacchino i suoi coralli, il fumo
par ne vibri sui tetti. Suore, uscite
senza le collegiali, stanno
su un greppo come capre: persi volti
chini su persi fiori.

A GIOVANNA, SULLE CAPRE

Non che non sono cattivose le capre di Dalpe.
Più che la voglia ingorda e l'anima vagabonda
saggezza le sospinge nei luoghi
più solivi della nostra conca
quando l'inverno è quasi senza neve,
e in giorni come questo luminosi,
vedi, non hanno corpo, non sono che macchie
nere sul greppo; e quella, immota contro il cielo,
potremo attraversarla tenendoci per mano.

LETTER FROM BELLINZONA

A bundle of years, a hill.
And the tallest castle.
All the gray as high as the doves,
all the green flowing up to the gray . . .
But today, without desire, with you
inside my wallet like an icon,
with immense pleasure I follow
the green path of a shooting star,
cast from the hand of a boy
stopped halfway up the Cockaigne
pole, satisfied
just to sit there. The rosy air
gathering in his shirt,
bit by bit the vesper
pours it over all the hill.
A turkey cries its chorus, smoke
seems to vibrate on the roofs. Nuns, out
without their boarders, stand
on a crag like nanny-goats: lost faces
bowed over lost flowers.

TO GIOVANNA, ON THE GOATS

No, it's not that the goats of Dalpe are mean.
More than their engorged desire and vagabond soul
it's wisdom drives them to the most sunlit
spots of our valley
when the winter's almost snowless,
and on bright days like this,
see, they have no body, they're just black
dots on the slope; and that one, still against the sky,
we can catch her, grabbing each others' hands.

Presto esulti, le chiami, gli porti fili d'erba,
lasci che l'una o l'altra ti venga a trovare,
e mentre t'annusa le tocchi il piccolo campano
che suona leggero ma franco più delle campanelle
dell'albero di Natale.

Guardala bene negli occhi, osserva
la tenace pupilla, e come (non piangere, non vanno)
a una giusta distanza ci circondano
e pregano per noi.

SINOPIE

> *. . . mentre in disparte l'umiltà dei vinti . . .*
> C. Rebora, Framm. XXXIV

Ce n'è uno, si chiama, credo, Marzio,
ogni due o tre anni mi ferma che passo
adagio, in bicicletta, dal marciapiede mi chiede
se Dante era sposato e come si chiamava sua moglie.
"Gemma", dico, "Gemma Donati." "Ah, sì, sì, Gemma",
fa lui, con suo sorriso, "grazie, mi scusi."
                                    Un altro,
più vecchio, che incontro più spesso, son sempre io a salutarlo
per primo, e penso: forse si ricorda
d'avermi aiutato, una notte di pioggia e di vento ch'ero uscito
per medicine, a rimettermi in sesto con suoi ferri (a quell'ora!)
una ruota straziata dall'ombrello.
Un terzo, quasi centenario, sordo, per solito
se appena mi vede grida: "Uheilà, giovinotto", e dal gesto si capisce
che mi darebbe, se potesse, una pacca paterna sulla spalla,
ma talora si limita a sorridermi, o, ad un tratto, eccitato

In no time you're excited, calling them, bearing blades of grass,
letting one or two come over to you, and
she nuzzles you as you flick her little bell
that sounds thin but clearer than the jingles
on a Christmas tree.

Look her right in the eyes, notice
her tenacious stare, and how (don't cry, they won't go)
at just the right distance they surround us
and pray for us.

SINOPIAS

> . . . *while on the fringes, the humility of the defeated* . . .
> C. Rebora, Fragment XXXIV

There's one, who's called, I think, Marzio,
every two or three years he hails me as I go
by, slow, on my bike, from the sidewalk he asks me
whether Dante was married and what was his wife's name.
"Gemma," I say, "Gemma Donati." "That's right, Gemma, yes,"
he replies, with his smile, "Thanks! Sorry to trouble you."
                                        Another man,
older, whom I run into more often, I'm always the one
to say hello first, and I think: maybe he remembers
that night he helped me—in the rain and wind when I'd gone
out for medicine—with his tools (and at that hour!)
to repair a tire torn by my umbrella.
A third, almost a hundred, hard of hearing, as usual
as soon as he sees me yells: "Hey there, young man," and I can tell
from his look that he'd give me, if he could, a fatherly slap on the back,
but sometimes he just smiles, or suddenly, excited he

esclama: "Ha visto! La camelia è sempre la prima a fiorire",
o altro, secondo la stagione.
                          D'altri
pure vorrei parlare, che sono già tutti sinopie
(senza le belle beffe dei peschi dei meli)
traversate da crepe secolari.

"CERTO D'UN MERLO IL NERO . . ."

et già di là dal rio passato è 'l merlo
deh, venite a vederlo . . .
Petrarca, CV

Certo d'un merlo il nero
mazzo di fiori d'un rosso
sorpreso dalla morte
nel breve buio d'un sottopassaggio
l'indomani farfalla
enorme d'un nero
punteggiato di rosso
nessuna traccia del giallo aranciato
il terzo giorno crosta
sfaldantesi in squame
eczema dell'asfalto il quarto
girasole dai petali rari
raschietti di spazzacamino

MAI SCOMPARSO

così che di sull'orlo
più d'una nuova potè raccontarmi
lo spazzino-necroforo

exclaims: "See that! The camellia is always the first to bloom,"
and so on, according to the season.

There are others
I'd like to mention, who are all already sinopias
(without the mockery of peach trees or apple)
traversed by the traces of age.

"YES IT'S A BLACKBIRD'S BLACK . . ."

> *and already the blackbird's beyond the river*
> *Pray, come and see . . .*
> Petrarch, CV

Yes it's a blackbird's black
bunch of flowers of a red
surprised by death
in a tunnel's brief darkness
the next day a butterfly
enormous of a black
dotted with red
no trace of the yellow-orange
the third day a scab
flaking into scales
eczema of asphalt the fourth
a sunflower with sparse petals
a chimney sweep's scrapers

JAMÁS DESAPARECIDO

so that over on the roadside
he could tell me a thing or two
the street sweeper-grave digger

esperto solo di trasmutazioni
rapide
      e in un mattino
pareva lentamente incenerirsi
ma nei fiati di nebbia del ritorno
ancora suppurava
toccati di bianco volani andavan variando
protesi verso piogge
sottili, già primaverili

ditelo ai merli sui marmi invernali
prima che i fiori del diavolo
moltiplichino il becco
delirino azalee

LE FORSIZIE DEL BRUDERHOLZ

> *Nimm die Forsythien tief in dich hinein*
> G. Benn, "Letzter Frühling"

Forse triste non è la pasquetta
del bianco drappello di Schwestern
che a mezzodì davanti all'ospedale
si riposano al sole di un'estate
precoce, tra soffi improvvisi di silfi
malefici, e quasi le avvolge
folta una gioia gialla di forsizie
attutita da merli perfetti

              (oh, nessuna
nelle notti di guardia quando si fa più vivo
il niente aiuterà

expert only in rapid
transmutations
                    and one morning
seemed to slowly turn to ash
but in the bursts of fog on the way back
festered still
touched with white the wheels went rushing
straining toward the thin
rains of early spring

warn the blackbirds on the winter marbles
before the devil's flowers
multiply their beaks before
azaleas rave

THE FORSYTHIAS OF BRUDERHOLZ

> *Take the forsythias deep inside yourself*
> G. Benn, "Final Spring"

Maybe Easter Monday's not sad
for the white squad of *Schwestern*
who at noon outside the hospital
rest in the sun of an early
summer, with sudden gusts of wicked
sylphs, almost enveloped in a
thick yellow joy of forsythias
subdued by perfect blackbirds

                    (oh, none
of the nights on vigil when the nothingness
makes itself most felt will help

con dosi improprie, eccessive, mortali
—d'insulina o sonnifero che astuto
si disperda nel corpo senza lasciarvi traccia,
o altro, aria iniettata nelle vene,
trasfusioni di sangue infetto, e in caso di coma
versare acqua nella gola schiacciando la lingua
con un cucchiaio perché finisca nei polmoni—
pazienti forse impazienti, forse bisognosi
di cure intense, lungodegenti
come si dice o terminali, ad andarsene in breve
ossia con sbrigativa sepoltura
dal mondo! nessuna farà
che questa dovizia di fiori e d'uccelli
si scandalizzi d'essere!)

                        e là, quanto basta in disparte
dentro a un vasto biancore di pietra
intorno a una fontana, una giovane, bionda
come d'inesperienza del male, come
lasciata in pace dall'eternità,
da poco s'è sdraiata con l'unico infermiere,
s'è tolta senza fretta le calze, fissa con occhi azzurrissimi
l'acqua, allunga un candido piede tranquillo
fino a sfiorare uno zampillo, parla,
forse parla d'amore

with incorrect, excessive, lethal doses
—of insulin or sedatives that slyly
disperse in the body without a trace,
or else, air injected into a vein,
transfusions of infected blood, or with comas
pouring water in the throat and holding down the tongue
so that it enters the lungs—
patients perhaps impatient, perhaps in need of
intensive treatments, chronic,
as they say, or terminal, soon to leave—
that is, with a hasty burial—
this world! none of them will make it
so that this abundance of flowers and of birds
is scandalized to exist!)

                  and there, just distant enough
in a vast whiteness of stone
around the fountain, a girl, blonde
as if from inexperience of suffering, as
if eternity had left her in peace, has
just lain down with the lone nurse,
leisurely removed her stockings, staring with the bluest eyes
at the water, extending a candid calm foot
to toe one of the jets, is speaking
maybe speaking about love

IN MEMORIA

Tornavo per farmi cambiare
il nastro ormai privo d'inchiostro
della mia vecchia Olivetti, e allungando,
come faccio, passando in bicicletta
davanti al tuo negozio, l'occhio
di là dai vetri, ho visto
che non c'era nessuno (forse
Lina è di sopra con Dora)
e ho visto CHIUSO PER LUTTO (forse
è morto Lino): da un po'
non ti vedevo, non mi contavi storielle.
Volevo dirti che mi sono accorto
solo adesso della totale scomparsa,
a sinistra, di E, di O a destra.
Il tasto è nero ma sempre lucente,
se batto (eternamente con due dita) continuo
a vederle, bianchissime, intatte
o quasi, come, là in basso, la x.

DA MOLTI ANNI

Da molti anni mio padre
non ha più sete.
O forse dura tuttavia.
"Io berrei l'universo" diceva al tempo del fieno.
Era certo una sete esagerata,
una cosa da canto trentesimo
dell'*Inferno* o tredicesimo della
Liberata.

IN MEMORY

I came back to replace
the now inkless ribbon
of my old Olivetti, and looking,
as I do, riding my bike
past your shop,
into the window, I saw
that no one was there (maybe
Lina's upstairs with Dora)
and I saw: CLOSED FOR MOURNING (maybe
Lino died): it had been a while
since I'd seen you, heard one of your stories.
I wanted to tell you that only now did I
realize the complete disappearance,
on the left, of the E, and O, on the right.
The keys are black but still shiny,
when I type (with two fingers, as always) I keep
seeing them, bright white, intact
or almost, just like, on the bottom, the x.

FOR YEARS

For years now my father's
thirst is gone.
Or perhaps it endures still.
"I could drink the universe," he'd say at hay time.
Sure, it was an exaggerated thirst
something out of the thirty-first
canto of the *Inferno* or the thirteenth
of the *Liberata*.

Non so figurarmi mio padre
in nessuno dei regni cosiddetti
d'oltretomba, non so fino a che punto
c'entri la sete, quella sua sete
di sceriffo insidiato da stanchezze
mortali verso l'ora di cena
quando era meglio non venirlo a trovare,
non chiedergli nulla, lasciarlo riposare.

I can't picture my father
in any of the so-called realms
of the hereafter, I can't figure out what
thirst has to do with it, that thirst he had
like a sheriff beset by mortal
fatigue come supper time
when it was better not to approach him,
not to ask him anything, to let him rest.

JR

REMO FASANI

IL FIUME

Il fiume . . . la mia infanzia n'era tutta
vinta. Veniva di lontano e andava
lontano. E mi affacciavo al suo mistero,
a quel suo mondo che mi rivelava
la vita accesa istante per istante.

Una bolla, e la seguo con il fiato
sospeso, vedo che si frange a un gorgo,
o ristà, prigioniera, dietro un sasso,
o si allontana e perde. Poi mi volto,
ne cerco e seguo un'altra, ancora un'altra.

Il fiume era le stagioni, l'anno.
In crescita e turbato da principio,
poi ricolmo, sospeso a cielo e nuvole,
poi fondo limpido a se stesso, agli altri,
infine vetro, anche senza gelo.

Ma più era le piene, le alluvioni.
Un giorno o due di furia . . . Poi la calma,
il ritorno alla norma e lo stupore
di non trovarla. Il fiume ora appariva
un altro, aveva dislocato tutto.

E qualche cosa andava dislocandosi,
ora, in chi lo guardava. E non soltanto
per lo sfacelo: per la trama tenera
su certe sabbie prima inesistenti.
La grazia ch'era al fondo della furia.

REMO FASANI

THE RIVER

The river . . . it completely conquered
my childhood. It came from afar and went
far away. And I faced its mystery,
its world that revealed to me
life activated moment by moment.

A bubble, and I follow it with bated
breath, I see it break against an eddy,
or return, trapped, behind a rock,
or drift off and disappear. Then I turn,
I find and follow another, and another.

The river was the seasons, the year.
Surging and turbulent at the start,
then full, up to the sky and clouds,
then a bottom clear to itself, to others,
finally glass, even without frost.

But it was more the highs, the floods.
A day or two of rage . . . Then the calm,
the return to normal and the surprise
at not finding it. Now the river seemed
like another, everything had shifted.

And some things were shifting,
now, in the one watching. And not only
from the decline: from the faint pattern
on certain sands before nonexistent.
The grace at the bottom of the rage.

JR

GIOVANNI ORELLI

DET DUMEGNA

U piasé da pissè can' la vissìa l'é piéna.
Pus a l'üss 't l'us'tarìa,
cun un pè sül s'c'aléuru
e l'autru sü la s'trèda 't l'ört,
us pissa senza préssa
cuntra 'l mü c''us das'créda
par via di c'èuri i invern l'aqua i s'tratemp
tücc i pissèt di chi 't la mura
mort e vivent, a l'us'tarìa:

u piasé da pissè senza l'umbrìa
d'un paisséi s'us farà la lüna o 'l vent,
pal lündas'dì o i tusèi
c''i pàssan sül s'c'aléuru cuntra l'üss
pòri piòi piü sül sö cume se iö
ui füss, quarciù da la sò man,
u Diàuru:

u piasé da pissè can c''u s'é tiss
e u vin a una bona misüra
e u s'as s'tüdia la bissa
c''la va verz l'insalata
e 'l su u sas sbassa dré i pitéi
"no, sulavévas mia tusèi,
u s'c'apa mia, i l'ò scè in man": e se
dopu 'na s'gorledìna cu la man
e gropù sü la pata,
s'us auza i öcc al s'tredón

GIOVANNI ORELLI

ON SUNDAY

The pleasure of pissing with a full vesica.
Near the door to the osteria
with one foot on the stair
and the other toward the field,
a piss without pressure
against the wall's crumbling plaster
'cause of the goats the water the rain the bad weather
all the piss of the people who've played morra
dead and alive, at the osteria:

the pleasure of pissing without a hint
of worry about the moon or the wind,
about next Monday or the girls
who pass down the stair by the exit,
poor little hens as rattled as if
it were, concealed behind my hand,
the Devil:

the pleasure of pissing when you're full
and wine flows in good measure
and you glance at the snake
heading for the greens
and the sun sets behind the roofs
"don't worry, ladies, it won't
escape, it's in hand": and
if after a little shake
you button your pants
and look up toward the main road

u fa piasé c'é cul pissè
l'öcc u s'é das'fesciù det tut chel tulbru
d'us'tarìa, det dumegna,
a prüma da nè int a dè fò i c'art
s'minè un tus c''u pedala in equilibriu
cume se mia c'aranz di c'èuri ma
ciuculatitt da mia s'c'üscè
ui füdess iö, par chi c'un vö, i la pulbra.

G'ASCIA

Vüna di chis'ti nocc det lüna,
vüna di chis'ti nef al lüm
du cel c'é i la campagna
la matin u pru l'é tampas'tù
di pass 't la vulp, di léuri, di föìt,
di bidri, 'mé biniss det infiniti
mis'teri gaudiosi gloriosi e dolorosi,
mila via mila avemarì
passéi i ni dit det föman
nècc i l'eternitè:

vüna di chisti nòcc c''u g'èra
u büi, u puz di rèi, e 'l rì ma
sot a la g'ascia l'aqua
cume s' la passess g'ü in padüra
la cur: la trüta
la s tira int i la vita
la s fa int i la tana
in u prufunt 't la tèra,
in u centru du munt:

what a pleasure that with pissure
the eye is cleared of all that muck
from the osteria, on Sunday,
and before going in to deal the cards
you see a boy pedaling with care
as if it weren't goat turds
but chocolates not to be crushed
there, for the taking, in the dirt.

ICE

One of these moonlit nights,
one of these snows in the light
of the sky in the countryside
in the morning the field is trampled
with footprints of foxes, hares, martens,
ermines, like beads of infinite
mysteries: joyful, sorrowful, glorious,
a thousand Vias, Ave Marias,
counted by the fingers of women
now passed on to eternity:

one of these nights that freezes
the fountain, the frog pond, the river
but under the ice the water
as if descending barefoot
flows: the trout
pulls itself into life
nestles into its lair
in the depths of the earth,
in the center of the world:

vüna di chis'ti lün c''la g'ascia
la incòla l'üss al limadè
e u g'èra u fièt süi vidri
ma i c'è i la nocc i dòrman
in fila sü la s'trèda'
'mé i mort du sciminteri:

ò insögnù una braméra
ò insgönù da basàt
e c'é u frecc u g'iaréva
vüna a l'autra i noss bocch,
e c'é par dag'arài
ui vaséva s'peciè la prümavera
ma c'é la prümavera
la ven dumà a la fin du munt
u dì du balurdon, det l'ira,
c'é i bocch di mort i mòrdan
tramurent i l'invern det Giosafat
u confiteor di culp, u rogaturus
al giüst c''u vegnarà sül rüss du munt,
'me 'l lüf dal bòsc', da Giüdas,
e intant 'na nüra
neira cun int un pien
det saèt e 't tampes't
. . . .
o dag'arài mèi piü,
mòrt
in u nota du Nota.

one of these moons that the ice
sticks the door to its frame
and freezes our breath on the windows
but at night the houses sleep
in a row on the street
like the dead in the cemeteries:

I dreamed of the hoarfrost
I dreamed of kissing you
and that the cold froze
our mouths together,
and that to unfreeze them
we had to wait for spring
but that spring
won't come till the end of the world
on the upside-down Dies Irae
when the mouths of the dead bite,
trembling, in the winter of Jehoshaphat
confiteor of sins, the *rogaturus,*
the righteous one who will come to the trash heap of the world,
like the wolf from the woods, the Judge,
and meanwhile a black
cloud carrying a load
of thunderbolts and storms
. . . .
or never to unfreeze them again,
death
in the absence of Absence.

JR

ELIO SCAMARA

AQUA SÓRGÌVA

L'é ent pen um cröis frèsć,
um bott cóme náá ent pen na gesa.
Er nona l'avress impieniid er ör del scòssáá
da ròdiiö er àqua ar bóca.
Mi am insginüügia
um bott cóme etnánz al Signór.
Agh daaǵ là ai cavill e al südóó.
A faaǵ un alt sègn . . . inària
cóme a casciáá un taramüüsc.
Am coota cón tüta er sèd,
a cón tütt el respètt,
intánt ch'i gótt sgèld
i batt sur sćèna bióta.

ELIO SCAMARA

THE SPRING

It's in a deep, cool valley,
a little like going into a church.
My nonna would use her apron
to bring the water to her mouth.
I get down on my knees,
as if before the Lord.
I run my hand over my hair and brow.
I make another sign . . . in the air
as if brushing away a spider web.
I kneel with all my thirst,
with all respect,
as the ice-cold drops
hit my naked back.

ER MÁGN

Cór nona
um bevèva dal scossáá.
Cór máma:
dai mai metüü inssèma a squèla.
El pà
ugh fèva mèèt er mágn vèrta cóntra er crèsta,
—dopo vèèla netàda via—
e ti sciüsciàva tra el dedómm a el signánd.

Pöö,
um scapàva da par nói ar fontàna:
agh èva sempru una mágn
ch'la fèèva i circol per àqua.

HAND

With Nonna
we drank from her apron.
With Mamma:
from her cupped hands.
Papa
had us each place a hand against the rock
—once they were clean—
and you slurped from the crook of your thumb.

Then,
we ran off to the fountain alone:
there was always a hand
making circles in the water.

JR

GRYTZKO MASCIONI

LANCEOLATE AGHIFORMI

Lanceolate aghiformi lineari
trafitture dell'aria:
lo sai che l'erba cipressina cresce
altissima fra pietre disastrose?
Lo sai che l'erba limoncina spreme
un'essenza d'aroma? E balsamita
dei crisantemi, o *vulgo*, di san Pietro,
è buona all'uso amabile che molce
anche i piatti più amari?
                                Non è che l'ombra
di una scienza, e impari
le forme del catalogo più lievi,
le più facili al mondo a trasalire,
a morire in un soffio
d'impazienza.
Ma dal niente del fossile di un fiore,
dal segno di una foglia puoi dedurre
l'immensa prateria che trascolora
al vento di un sorriso che non muove
dal quel suo punto immemore
nel tempo:
e tanto basta—irrigidito ardore—
a risarcire il troppo
del dolore.
(Lo sai che l'erba medica è foraggio
per il nostro coraggio,
che ci vendica tacita del male
nel silenzio che sale?)

GRYTZKO MASCIONI

LANCEOLATE ACIFORMS

Straight lanceolate aciform
spikes in the air:
did you know that cypress spurge grows
tallest between disastrous rocks?
Did you know that lemon balm exudes
aromatic essence? And balsam
herb, or in *vulgo*, St. Peter's herb,
amiably serves to sweeten
even the most bitter dishes?
                                    It's simply the shadow
of a science, and you learn
the wispiest forms in the catalogue,
the world's most prone to startle,
to fall dead in a huff
of impatience.
But from the trifle of the fossil of a flower,
from the imprint of a leaf you can sense
the immense meadow that changes color
in the breeze of a smile that never moves
from its immemorial point
in time:
and that much is enough—rigid ardor—
to mend the excess
of pain.
*(Do you know that alfalfa is forage
for our courage,
that avenges us, tacit, from faults
in the silence that assaults?)*

SCUSA IL DISTURBO

Scusa il disturbo ma risulta ai fatti
che questa voce è quella di un poeta
che sa la verità per dismisura
dell'usura del cuore o dei misfatti
del quotidiano (non importa), importa
che tu mi ascolti:
non soffrire; sciolti
vanno ringhiando i cani della notte
e ci oscurano il giorno
di latrati.
Tu non soffrire:
non ostruire i fiumi che del mare
cercano il sale,
lasciali andare liberi al prescelto
delirio e scegli solo di guardare,
in un taglio di sole,
di tacere.

Venezia, 30 gennaio 1981

PARLARE DEI PAESI

a Felice Menghini, in memoria

Un invito a parlare dei paesi
mi sollecita amico:
ma che non sia memoria calpestata
ogni nome randagio alla memoria,
mi dico in questa nuvola di lutto
o incivile diaspora

PARDON THE INTERRUPTION

Pardon me if I interrupt but it's evident
that this is the voice of a poet
who knows the truth by surfeit
of overuse of the heart or the misdeeds
of the everyday (no matter), it matters
that you hear me:
do not suffer; unleashed
the dogs of the night go growling
and darken our day
with howls.
Do not suffer:
don't dam the rivers that seek
the salt of the sea,
let them go free to their chosen
delirium and choose just to watch,
in a swath of sunlight,
to be silent.

Venice, January 30, 1981

ABOUT OUR TOWNS

To Felice Menghini, in memory

A friendly voice urges me
to speak about our towns:
but it can't be a memory trampled,
every name stray to memory,
I tell myself in this cloud of mourning
or uncivil diaspora

del cuore. Sapevamo i sentieri
e uno per uno
i nomi delle capre dispettose,
ma non sia mai pretesto rusticano
a una fuga nel vano, se imperversa
il testo dei poeti travestiti,
con gli slogan falliti dei profeti,
—osceno minuetto, esca perversa—
sottobanco pagati, alibi ciechi
al nefando persistere del tutto.
Io che vengo dai monti abiterò
le vagabonde isole del cielo,
care ultime luci
intermittenti
di un pensiero precario: e scorderò
la discorsiva tenerezza il cupo
rimbombare del tuono tra le valli
(ma il cuore torna inerme dove piove
eternamente su quei fuochi antichi
di castagne arrostite, di arrossite
ragazze al primo bacio,
e piango
fango).

Origlio, lunedì di Pasqua, 1979

of the heart. We knew the trails
and the names
of each and every ornery goat,
but it can't be a rustic excuse
to drift into trifles, if it perverts
the words of poets in disguise,
with the failed slogans of the prophets,
—obscene minuet, perverse bait—
paid under the table, alibis blind
to the nefarious persistence of everything.
I who come from the mountains will inhabit
the wandering islands of the sky,
dear last lights
intermittent
with a precarious thought: and I'll forget
the soft speech the deep
rumble of the thunder through the valleys
(but the heart returns defenseless where it rains
eternally on the ancient fires
of roasted chestnuts, of flushed
girls at the first kiss,
and mud I
cry).

Origlio, Easter Monday, 1979

JR

ALBERTO NESSI

DUE POESIE PER LA GATTA

La scomparsa

Della sua vita è rimasto poco: il pannello di pavatex
graffiato dalle unghie, il fantasma che torna ogni sera
quando ci pare di vederla tra i gerani, i racconti
delle sue imprese tra le piante grasse
piroette passi di carica balletti con le mosche,
la rivalità con gli altri gatti che noi scacciavamo
quasi lei fosse d'un'altra razza felina
e non una bastardella gentile. Della vita
rimangono solo tracce e fantasmi.
Una gatta come lei
o l'hanno avvelenata con la meta
o l'uomo della fattoria l'ha scuoiata per mangiarla:
ma se fosse scappata di casa, adolescente in cerca d'amore,
e la rivedessimo domani immobile
al centro della terrazza
a proteggere le nostre vite ugualmente precarie?

Il ritorno

Proprio il giorno della mia profezia.
È stato facile credere al poeta, meno facile
vederla aggirarsi storta per la casa. Non pareva più lei
vecchia e senza gusto per le farfalle notturne
passata improvvisamente dalla fanciullezza alla quiescenza
se tentava un salto le zampe dietro
si sgangheravano: aveva preso una legnata?
Voleva nascondersi, rasentava i muri
come tutti gli storpi, gli spaventati.

ALBERTO NESSI

TWO POEMS FOR THE CAT

The Disappearance

Little is left of her life: the fiberboards
scratched by her claws, the ghost that appears every night
when we think we spot her in the geraniums, the stories
of her adventures through the succulents,
the pirouettes, sprints, ballet dances with flies,
the rivalry with the other cats we'd shoo away
as if she were another breed of cat
and not a mongrel of gentle birth. Of her life
only traces and ghosts remain.
With a cat like her
either she was poisoned on purpose
or some peasant skinned and ate her—
but what if she ran away from home, a young girl looking for love,
and we saw her tomorrow immobile
in the middle of the terrace
protecting our equally precarious lives?

The Return

The very day I'd predicted.
It had been easy to trust the poet, not so easy
to see her hobbling around the house. She didn't seem herself
aged and listless with moths
gone suddenly from girlhood to quiescence
if she attempted a jump her back legs
buckled: had she taken a beating?
She wanted to hide: she hugged the walls
like all the crippled, the frightened.

DONNA IN UN CORTILE

C'è una donna rinchiusa in un cortile
d'asfalto, dietro il cancello
saluta con cenni di mano ammiccando
nella faccia colore della terra,
la domenica dà un bacio a mia figlia
vestita d'azzurro come un settembrino.
Quante volte mi ha detto che passa gli ottanta?
Che una volta le gambe erano buone, che andava
scalza a portare gerlate di grassa?
Dice a tutti "cara", vuol parlare un po'
calata qui dai monti di Roncapiano
dove non è rimasto più nessuno
—la scuola deserta, muti di vacche
i pascoli, precipitati
in fondo alle gole i giorni dell'aquilegia.
Un mattino la vedo senza grembiule, felice
nelle sue scarpe di vero cuoio
avventurarsi fino alla Farmacia
fuori del mondo, là, sulla cantonale.

WOMAN IN A COURTYARD

There's a woman enclosed in an asphalt
courtyard, behind the gate she
waves hello with a wink,
her face the color of the earth;
on Sundays she gives a kiss to my daughter
dressed in blue like an aster.
How many times has she told me she's over eighty?
That her legs used to be good, that she would
go barefoot to haul baskets of manure?
She calls everyone "dear," she likes to chat,
landed here from the Roncapiano mountains
where no one lives anymore
—the school deserted, the pastures
soundless of cows, the days of the columbines
plunged to the bottom of the ravines.
One morning I see her apronless, happy
in her genuine leather shoes
venturing all the way to the pharmacy
outside the world, there, on the boulevard.

JR

AURELIO BULETTI

"STAMANI…"

Stamani
di buona voglia
ci mettemmo a godere
il vento, la tempesta e la sua festa
il sasso nello stagno, l'arc-en-ciel
il giorno intercalare
che già di-g-rada
stasera.

UN LIEVE SEGNO

Beati i ricchi
che popolano il lago
di vele bianche:
che le sospinga il vento fino a sera
ti terrò fra le braccia sulla riva:
se di loro sarà qualsiasi regno
di noi non resterà che un lieve segno
tanto dolce fu il giorno, tanto alto.

BAR MONTI

Seduti a un tavolino,
manchevoli di briciole,
nulla donammo ai passeri chiedenti:
fu il loro un iter di sola speranza.

AURELIO BULETTI

"THIS MORNING…"

This morning
in good spirits
we went to relish
the wind, the tempest and its feast
the pebble in the pond, the *arc-en-ciel*
the intercalary day
already de-clin-ing
tonight.

A FAINT TRACE

Blessed are the rich
who fill the lake
with their white sails:
may the wind push them till dusk
I'll hold you in my arms on the shore:
if any kingdom shall be theirs
only a faint trace of us will remain
so sweet was the day, so bright.

BAR MONTI

Sitting around a table,
without the slightest crumb,
we gave the begging sparrows nothing:
theirs were the motions of mere hope.

28.2.

Nevica
nel bianco si riposa, lievemente
l'amorosa, l'inquieta che chiamiamo
vita.

POESIA SPICCIA

La gioia è proletaria,
ricca soltanto
di ciò che mette al mondo,
il dolore è borghese,
ha sempre qualche entrata.

RIVALITÀ

Capita che chi scrive si scoraggi
e si stizzisca per la tenuità
in cui sono viventi le parole
e invidi a chi dipinge
la sostanza dell'olio.

2/28

Snowing
in the white she rests, light,
the unquiet lover we call
life.

COIN-POEM

Joy is proletarian,
rich only
with what it gives to the world,
pain is bourgeois,
it always has some income.

RIVALRY

Sometimes a writer gets discouraged
bothered by the tenuousness
in which words dwell
and envies those who paint
the substance of oil.

JR

DONATA BERRA

MAGICA

A frammenti, solo
e per ellissi
risponde
la biblioteca della memoria.

Alla richiesta, all'urgenza del prestito
(e lo struggimento dell'ora vorrebbe
subito, qui, tutto, il passato
per colmare il dolore
e garantirlo)

lievemente
come galleggiano i sogni
dall'aria insondabile del remoto
innalza un'immagine

onnipotente, illustrata e magica.

TENTANDO

Tentando di uscire dal porto
gli incagli erano questi, nominabili:
gòmene draghe gru gialle
argani ruggini, rostri
scialuppe appese a corde
Maria, di sguincio, addossata a un palo.

DONATA BERRA

MAGIC

In fragments, only
and in ellipses
the library of memory
responds.

At the request, the urgency of the loan
(and the longing of the moment wants
the past, now, here, complete,
to fill in the pain
and ensure it)

softly
the way that dreams float
with the unfathomable air of the remote
rises an image:

omnipotent, illuminated, magic.

TRYING

Trying to leave the port
the obstacles, identifiable, were these,
hawsers, dredges, yellow cranes,
rust capstans, cutwaters
lifeboats hanging on ropes
Maria, aslant, leaning against a pole.

La mano già sulla barra del timone
sganciate le marre, ma
la città che fa da àncora
il vecchio suona e non ha più sentore
se non del cambio tra la notte e il giorno
come quell'altro suo compagno a prua
gli occhi d'acqua, la giacchetta lisa
con una rosa, rosa rossa in mano.

AL PORTO

Al porto, uno

A ridosso dell'onda, preso
tra le maglie della rete, perso
al finisterre sguardo, e le passioni:
fermo, aspettando che calino le nasse.

Al porto, due

Senza apparente scopo
come la lenta risacca

ma con visibile fastidio
per le frasi che non la riguardano

sta la bella donna
seduta al bar Blu Mare

attorcigliando il fumo
cilestrino della sigaretta.

Hand already at the helm
the flukes are unhooked, but
the city acts as an anchor
the old man sounds the horn, senses nothing
save the transition from night to day
like his partner over at the bow
his watery eyes, his threadbare coat
and a rose, a red rose, in his hand.

AT THE PORT

At the Port, One

Sheltered by the wave, caught
in the weave of the net, lost
gaze at land's end, and passions:
still, waiting for the keepnets to drop.

At the Port, Two

Without an apparent purpose
like the slow undertow,

but with visible irritation
at the phrases disregarding her

is the beautiful woman
sitting at the Blu Mare bar

the pale blue smoke
of her cigarette coiling.

LUI

Avevano un bell'offrirgli ex voto
erigere tempietti innumeri chiesette
cappelle a picco sugli scogli, nicchie
a perpendicolo sul mare: lui

lui che sarebbe il loro protettore
il solo patrono loro accreditato
Aghios Eolios, santo e pescatore

lui non riuscivano mai a prenderlo.

Così con quel poco sego
prima che fosse alba
gli accendevano smilze candeline
gialle, infilzate fuori
nella sabbia, in riva, ma lui
lui era già sul mare
già sul mare aperto
a spaziare, che alcuni
credono di poter dire, e pensare
che lui
è lo stesso come le schiene
per gioco curve dei delfini,
lui già svagava basso sulle curve onde, svariava
radente a braccia spalancate, a rondine
non a croce, no, sfiorante
il mare che non finisce.

Altri fermi sulla riva di un grande Egeo
dicevano che
quando tutti son via e

HE

Indomitable they brought him ex-votos
erected countless temples churches
chapels on the peaks of cliffs
hanging over the sea: he

he, their would-be protector
the only patron they were given
Aghios Eolios, fisherman and saint

they never managed to catch him.

So with their little tallow
before day broke
for him they lit thin candles,
yellow, sticking out
of the sand, on the shore, but he
he was already on the sea
already on the open sea
roaming free, and some
think they can say, and believe
that he
is the arched backs
of dolphins at play, but he
was already oblivious low over the round waves, heedless
skimming with arms splayed, like a swallow,
not like a cross, no—grazing
the endless sea.

Others standing on the shore of the great Aegean
said that
when everyone is gone and

non c'è più nessuno
quel suono che si ascolta è il suo,
altri inviperiti lo vituperano
dicono, perfido! se ne stia
persino posato
sugli spilli di punta delle ali
alle rondini di mare.

no one is around
that sound you hear is him,
others enraged rage against him
saying, that jerk! I hope
he hits
the tips of the sea
swallows' wings.

JR

ANTONIO ROSSI

SPALATORI DI NEVE

Gli spalatori di neve, puliti i gradini della sinagoga,
si incamminano verso altri piazzali,
sorpassano fischiando motivi
una comitiva di sciatori attardati.
Sembrano quasi una processione,
col loro portamento e con quelle pale quadrate e nere
alzate sulle spalle a mo' di gonfalone;
quand'ecco che dal drappello finora unito
se ne stacca uno, più esile e silenzioso,
e mentre gli altri procedono imperturbati
egli tentenna prima, poi imbocca una via laterale
scomparendo quasi subito fra le reti e i sempreverdi.

ANTONIO ROSSI

SNOW SHOVELERS

The snow shovelers, having scraped the synagogue steps,
move on to other public places,
whistling catchy tunes, they overtake
a party of belated skiers.
With their festive bearing and square black shovels
carried over their shoulders like banners,
they seem almost a procession.
Then from the so far united troop
one frailer and quieter suddenly breaks away,
and while the others proceed unperturbed
he first hesitates then makes off down a side street
vanishing almost immediately among fences and evergreens.

SK

FABIO PUSTERLA

LE PARENTESI

L'erosione
cancellerà le Alpi, prima scavando valli,
poi ripidi burroni, vuoti insanabili
che preludono al crollo, gorghi. Lo scricchiolio
sarà il segnale di fuga: questo il verdetto.
Rimarranno le pozze, i montaruzzi casuali,
le pause di riposo, i sassi rotolanti,
le caverne e le piane paludose.
Nel Mondo Nuovo rimarranno, cadute
principali e alberi sintattici, sperse
certezze e affermazioni,
le parentesi, gli incisi e le interiezioni:
le palafitte del domani.

IL DRONTE

E se le sprofondanti immensità temevi
sopra o sotto, i marosi o il vento,
riparo le rocce ancora erano, alla novità ventosa,
allo spruzzo, all'orrore del fondo.
Era un regno di basalto, precipizio
su raggrumate colate di lava, su smangiati coralli.
Ma poi: un luccichio di sestanti, cannocchiali.
Abbattute le foreste piantarono canne da zucchero.
E tu inerte zampettante
prigioniero dell'isola, schiacciato
fra due azzurri diversi, di inesausta durezza.
E muri ciechi, di vele spiegate su caracche, e bandiere,
fiocchi, pappafichi, tonfi d'ancora. E ghigni
di topi, pipistrelli, camaleonti e gechi.

FABIO PUSTERLA

PARENTHESES

Erosion
will erase the Alps, first scoring valleys,
then deep ravines, bottomless pits
foreshadowing the collapse, chasms. A groaning
will be the signal for flight: this the verdict.
Left will be pools, chance mounds,
pauses for rest, erratic boulders,
caves and marshy plains.
In the New World, after the fall
of syntax trees and main clauses, the loss
of certainties and affirmations, left will be
parentheses, incidentals, and interjections:
the pile-works of tomorrow.

THE DODO

And if you feared the giddying immensity
above or below, breeze or breaker,
the rocks were still your refuge from what the wind might bring,
the spray, the horror of the deep.
Yours was a kingdom of basalt, high above
clotted lava flows, rolled and eroded coral.
But then: the glint of sextant and spyglass.
The forests felled, they planted sugarcane.
And you, indolent plodder,
prisoner of the island, trapped
between blue and blue, each of unyielding hardness.
And blind walls, of canvas spread on carracks, and flags,
staysails, top-gallants, the splash of anchors. And the jeers
of rats, bats, chameleons, and geckos.

"SE POTESSI SCEGLIERE . . ."

Se potessi scegliere un gesto, un luogo e un'ora,
l'ora sarebbe una sera d'aria tesa
e il luogo sarebbe un luogo come tanti:
una baracca in curva,
una pausa appena accennata di qualcosa,
calda bassa e fumosa,
dove seduto a un tavolo, toccando
una spalla, una mano o un bicchiere,
prenderei tempo prima di alzarmi
a seguire qualche sconosciuto fuori.

"E POI QUALCUNO VA . . ."

E poi qualcuno va, tutto è più vuoto.
Se ci ritroveremo, sarà per non conoscerci,
diversi nei millenni, nella storia
faticosa di tutti; e intanto arretrano
i ghiacciai, s'inghiotte il mare
lo stretto, ed il passaggio
è già troppo profondo, impronunciabile,
sepolto nel passato il tuo viaggio. Se ci ritroveremo
non ci sarà memoria per me, insetto,
per te, fatto farfalla tropicale.
D'altra parte, lo sai, non ci vedremo
più. Nessun colombo verrà, nessuna pista
a ricucire lo strappo, la deriva
di morte.

"IF I COULD CHOOSE . . ."

If I could choose an action, place, and time,
the time would be an evening with tension in the air
and the place a place of no special distinction:
a shack on a bend,
a pause barely hinted at of something
hot low and smoky,
where, seated at a table, touching
a shoulder, hand, or glass,
I would take my time before getting up
and following some stranger outside.

"AND THEN SOMEONE GOES . . ."

And then someone goes, everything is emptier.
If we meet again, it will be without recognition,
different in the millennia, in the wearisome
history of us all, and meanwhile the ice floes
recede, the sea swallows up
the strait, and the pass
is already too deep, unpronounceable,
your crossing buried in the past. If we meet again
there will be no memory for me, insect,
for you, become a tropical butterfly.
In any case, you know, we shall not meet
again. No carrier pigeon* will come, no trail
to bridge again the rift, the drift
of death.

---

* The Italian *colombo* (pigeon) also alludes to Christopher Columbus, "discovering"
the land on the opposite shore of the Bering Strait, where once there was a land bridge
between the two continents.

ROGGIA

Passo di qui, tornando da un lungo viaggio,
come in un cimitero di memorie.
La pozzanghera c'è sempre, anche d'estate,
il fango, la sterrata, i ciuffi d'erba
e d'ortica non cambiano mai. Sassi e sterpaglie
spariranno anche loro, soffocati da una morsa
più forte, di cemento, un giorno o l'altro,
e forse prima ancora dei nostri ricordi;
ma per adesso ci sono, ed è il paesaggio
desolato che ho scelto per te. L'ultima casa
aperta al vento e alla luce, una pianura
quasi sempre deserta, non amena,
che percorre lentissima
una roggia. Io fumo, sto sul ponte,
e getto anche per te una sigaretta
nell'acqua scura. È un rito
senza senso, meno ancora che un rito:
un'abitudine. Già con mio padre, a volte, sotto i fiori;
e mi domando cosa avrà pensato mia madre
di quel tabacco tombale: spettri, vandali?
O forse ha indovinato e non ne parla
per pudore. Full flavor blend, comunque, una miscela
mediocre, piuttosto grezza, maryland: la sigaretta
rossa dei muratori, o così dicono. Anche il nome
riporta a sogni lisi e fuori corso: Parisienne,
ragazze che sgambettano su un palco al Moulin Rouge,
le luci di Pigalle, la naftalina di un secolo, BB.
O Jeanne Moreau, col suo volto
vastissimo e profondo: le sarebbe piaciuto
questo tabacco. Oggi però inattesi
dall'argine sono spuntati cinque germani

DRAINAGE DITCH

I come this way, back from a long journey,
as if in a graveyard of memories.
The puddle is still here, even in summer;
the mud, the cart track, the clumps of grass
and nettles never change. Stones and brushwood, too,
will disappear, crushed in a more constrictive vice
of cement, one day or another,
and maybe even sooner than our memories;
but for now they exist, and this is the desolate
landscape I have chosen for you. The last house
open to wind and sunlight, a flat expanse
almost always deserted, unprepossessing,
through which a sluggish canal
pursues its course. I stand on the bridge and smoke
and throw a cigarette into the dark water
for you, too. A senseless rite,
not even a rite: a habit.
Just as I did with my father, sometimes, under the flowers;
and I wonder what my mother must have thought
of that sepulchral tobacco: ghosts, vandals?
Or maybe she guessed but maintained a tactful
silence. Full flavor blend, though, a mediocre
mixture, rather rough, Maryland: the red
working man's smoke, or so they say. Even the name
begets worn and wasted dreams: *Parisienne*,
girls cavorting on stage at the Moulin Rouge,
the lights of Pigalle, a century in mothballs, BB.
Or the looming, thoughtful face of
Jeanne Moreau: she would have liked
this tobacco. Today, though, five mallards
suddenly emerged from the bank

spaventandomi quasi. Sono scesi in acqua regali,
risalendo la poca corrente della roggia, e uno di loro
si è voltato un istante.

LAMENTO DEGLI ANIMALI CONDOTTI AL MACELLO

Guarda: ci portano via. Nella canzone
dei giorni ci stramazzano. E cantiamo
per questa ultima ora: noi cantiamo
la nostra bellezza negata. E siamo vivi.

Vagano spore al vento, ali del cuore
che chiama il sangue a sé, che lo fa scorrere
nei fiumi delle vene, ai venti caldi
dei desideri che ci sono tolti. E siamo vivi.

E sono mari i nostri desideri,
percorriamo foreste di memoria
tra poco incenerite, ed ora splendide.

Cenere di tronchi, i mari in secca. Ma noi vivi,
vivi più vivi della mano che martoria. Chi ci nega
la luce ignora questo: siamo vivi

nella gloria del male che ci è dato,
nel silenzio del colpo che ci è inferto.
Muti, dimenticati.

almost scaring me. Regally, they dropped into the water,
swimming against the feeble current, and for an instant
one of them turned.

LAMENT OF THE ANIMALS TAKEN FOR SLAUGHTER

Look: they are taking us away. In the song
of the days they strike us down. And we sing
for this last hour: we sing
of our beauty denied. And we live.

Spores drift in the wind, wings of the heart
that calls the blood to itself, that makes it run
in the rivers of the veins, to the hot winds
of the desires taken from us. And we live.

And our desires are seas,
we roam forests of memory
soon to be reduced to ash, and now splendid.

Ash of tree trunks, the seas run dry. But we live,
alive more alive than the hand that tortures. He who denies us
the light is unaware of this: we live

in the glory of the evil done to us,
in the silence of the blow inflicted on us.
Mute, forgotten.

SK

PIETRO DE MARCHI

LE ROSE DELL'EROS

Come le rose del giardino
loro rosse sorelle
anche le rose dell'eros
dispongono di spine.

E allora ascolta Händel
e prima che sia sera
"lascia la spina,
cogli la rosa".

ASIMMETRIE

Chissà che cosa di noi due, di te
ricordo, che tu forse non ricordi;

chissà che cosa di noi due, di me
da tempo in me è perduto e in te perdura.

LA CATÒRBOLA

Come la serpe striscia
Nell'erba la catòrbola,
Ma non ti morde mica,
Non è una biscia biscia.

È come una lucertola che ha perso
Le zampe, e allora striscia.

PIETRO DE MARCHI

THE ROSE OF EROS

Like roses in the garden
their crimson sisters
the roses of eros
abound in thorns.

So listen, Händel,
and before it's late
"*lascia la spina,*
cogli la rosa."

ASYMMETRIES

Who knows what about us, about you
I remember, that you might not remember;

who knows what of us, about me
for a time is lost in me and in you will last.

THE SLOWWORM

Like the snake it slithers
In the grass: the slowworm.
But it certainly won't bite you,
It's not a snake snake, it squirms.

It's like a lizard that grew
No legs, and so it slithers.

ANCORA VERSO MARINA

Là dove l'altra estate fu un ramarro
la preda ignara di un giorno felice
pensi agli amori che durano più delle dune,
alla cicala che ricicla il suo canto,
tutti gli anni lo stesso.
Nel sole-ombra dei pini pare immune
dagli sgarbi del tempo
il tuo gusto feroce dell'estate.

AGAIN TOWARD MARINA

There where a green lizard lay last summer
prey unaware of a happy day
you think of loves that last longer than dunes,
of the cicada that recycles its song,
every year the same.
In the sunshade of the pines, seeming immune
to the incivilities of time,
your fierce hunger for summer.

JR

VANNI BIANCONI

LA CITTÀ SENZA ASSEDIO (*estratti*)

Mostar, Bosnia

Dal ponte ci accompagna alla sua stanza
lontana del centro quasi quanto sono stato
da questa e ogni guerra prima del ponte,
degli edifici forzati, piegati,
dei fori dentro i muri e sul suo braccio,
rimarginati, soffre solo il tempo quando cambia.
Forse non ho mai visto un fiume come questo
che per ogni corrente ha un nome e mai
la stessa direzione, e il terrazzamento
arabo di case cristiane, spiazzi, fronde.
Forse se non fosse ricostruito e calmo
e così familiare da sembrare
a un passo da casa ogni pezzo di casa
e la guerra lontana dodici anni
capirei ancora meno come insorge,
trama e si uccide eternamente
l'umanità, ma le parole in realtà
non sono separate dal reale
come lo sono i nomi sulla mappa
e se lui ha detto che è folle
tutto quello che è successo
questo conta più dell'odio che i tempi
potrebbero iniettare nei buchi del suo braccio.

Il suo cecchino si è suicidato, dice, non sa perché.

*

VANNI BIANCONI

from THE UNBESIEGED CITY

Mostar, Bosnia

From the bridge he leads us to his room
almost as far from town as I was
from this and every war before the bridge,
the forced, folded buildings,
the holes in the walls and his arm,
closed up, but he feels it with changing weather.
Maybe I've never seen a river like this one
that has a name for every current and never
the same direction, and the Arab terraces
with Christian houses, the clearings, foilage.
Maybe if it weren't rebuilt and calm
and so familiar that every piece of a home
seems close to home,
and if the war weren't twelve years past
I'd understand even less how humanity
eternally rebels, plots, and kills,
but in reality words
aren't separate from the real
like the names on the map
and if he said that everything
that happened is madness
it counts more than the hate that the changing times
could inject into the holes in his arm.

His sniper committed suicide, he says, he doesn't know why.

    *

Quello che sapevo della guerra
ha preso corpo con lui e i palazzi in pezzi,
tra le case rammendate con cura,
l'ha preso come il cancro prende il corpo,
è nella transizione che si coglie,
cosa può succedere a un uomo
nella transizione incredula alla guerra?
Quello che è successo sempre. Paura
di avvicinarmi a Sarajevo.
Colline, montagne, il fiume verde,
cumuli di fieno ovunque, vecchi seni
ancora pronti a dare latte, Oberland
islamico verso una Zurigo certa
di sopravvivere a se stessa. Sarajevo
in cui il cemento è cauto come garza
e niente sembra ricomposto per lotta
o progresso, ma perché torni la città
il cui seno insegna alle sue madri il latte.

What I knew about war
took shape with him and the buildings in bits,
among the houses mended with care,
it took shape like cancer takes the body,
it's in the transition that you understand
what can happen to a man
in the incredulous transition to war.
Same as always happens. Fear
of approaching Sarajevo.
Hills, mountains, the green river,
bales of hay everywhere, old breasts
still ready to give milk, a Muslim
Oberland leading to a Zurich so sure
of surviving itself. Sarajevo
where the concrete is fragile as gauze
and nothing seems recomposed for struggle
or progress, but for the return of the city
whose breast shows milk to its mothers.

JR

III
RHAETO-ROMANIC

TRANSLATED BY
DONAL MCLAUGHLIN,
WITH LINGUISTIC INPUT FROM
THE EDITOR

PEIDER LANSEL

FOSSAS A L'ESTER

Cun cipress chi perchüran sa quaidezza,
illa cretta dals vegls sta'l champ da pos.
Süls tömbels seis, tanter l'urbaj'ün vezza
blers noms dals noss.

Noms! . . . Be il marmel chi las fossas serra
tegn'adimmaint alchet dals trapassats.
Qua, sco'l Creader voul: "Da terr'in terra!"
tuots sun tuornats.

Chi sa dad els? Fidand in lur vantüra,
giuvnets amo sun its per il muond suot,
per subit s'inaccordscher: vita düra
es dapertuot.

Ant cha lur gran rivess a metter spias,
quel es stat tschunc tras ün crudel destin.
Oters, chi dvantenn vegls cun lur fadias,
qui'a la fin,

stanguels, han chattà pasch davo l'arsaja
vers la patria e'l lönch bramà success—
Morts invlidats, süls tömbels voss l'urbaja
nun as mangelss,

cha glori'uman'es propi main co nöglia!
Bellezza rösa, l'cuort flurir glivrà,
laschand crodar sül tömbel fögli'a föglia,
letta s'affà.

Sunteri protestant. Via Erbosa, Livorno, lügl 1938

PEIDER LANSEL

GRAVES ABROAD

Beneath the cypresses minding its silence
lies the Protestant cemetery.
On the tombs between the laurels
the names of our soldiers.

Names . . . Only the marble slabs
know about the dead.
Here, as our Creator wished—"Earth to earth!"
—all have returned.

Who knows them now?—Trusting their luck
they traveled the world in their youth
and soon learned that life everywhere
is hard.

The stalk had yet to ripen,
when fate mowed it down.
Others who, with troubles and cares, grew
old and weary,

worn down by longing for their homeland,
and striving for success, found peace here—
Forgotten dead, the laurels on your graves
are meaningless,

human glory is worth nothing! Less!
A beautiful rose that briefly blooms
then, petal by petal, wilts on your tomb
would better suit you.

Protestant cemetery. Via Erbosa, Livorno, July, 1938

TAMANGUR

Aintasom S-charl (ingio sun rafüdats
tuouts oters gods), sün spuonda vers daman,
schi varsaquants veidrischems dschembers stan
da vegldüm e strasoras s-charplinats.
Tröp sco l'ingual nu's chatta plü ninglur,
ultim avanz d'ün god dit: "Tamangur".

Da plü bodun quel sgüra cuvernet
costas e spis cha bluots uossa vezzain;
millieras d'ans passettan, e scumbain
ch'ardenn sajettas e cha naiv terret,
ha tantüna la vita gnü vendschur
e verdagià trasoura Tamangur.

Mo cur umbras l'uman gnit be sdrüand,
sainza ningün pisser sün il davo,
schi lavinas e boudas s'fettan pro.
L'ajer dvantet vieplü crüj, fintant
nu madürenn plü'ls bös-chs las puschas lur,
e daspö quai al main get Tamangur.

As dostand fin l'ultim, indavoman,
ils dschembers, ün ad ün, sco schlass sudats
chi sül champ da battaglia sun crodats,
per terra vi schmarscheschan plan a plan—
E scha l'agüd nu vain bainbod—Dalur!—
svanirà fin il nom da Tamangur.

Al veider god, chi pac a pac gnit sdrüt,
sumaglia zuond eir nos linguach prüvà,
chi dal vast territori d'üna jà

TAMANGUR

Right at the end of the Scarl Valley (where the forest
has otherwise gone) remain, on the eastern slope,
some ancient pines,
ravaged by time and many a storm.
A troop, the likes of which can nowhere else be found;
the last remains of a forest, called Tamangur.

Long ago, the forest covered no doubt
slopes and ridges, now laid bare;
thousands of years passed, lightning
may have struck and snow fallen,
yet life triumphed,
for all that time it was green, Tamangur.

But when man then came, and his greedy destruction,
not thinking of later,
so, too, did avalanches and mudflows.
The air became rawer and rawer,
the pine cones soon no longer ripened,
it was then it started to retreat, Tamangur.

The pines defended themselves to the last
falling, one by one, like brave warriors
on the battlefield.
Now, on the ground, they slowly rot.
And if help doesn't come—alas,
not just the name will fade: Tamangur.

The language we know and love,
forced back from a vast territory
to its current narrower confines

in uschè strets cunfins uoss'es ardüt.
Scha'ls Rumantschs nu fan tuots il dovair lur,
giaraj'a man cun el sco Tamangur.

Co invlidessans ch'el da seculs nan
savet noss vegls da redscher e guidar?
Ierta ch'adüna tgnettan adachar,
varguogna bain, sch'la dessans our da man.
Tgnain vi dal nos, sco'ls oters vi dal lur,
e'ns algordain la fin da Tamangur.

Be nö dar loc!—Ningün nu pudrà tour
a la schlatta rumantscha 'l dret plü ferm,
chi'd es quel: da mantgnair dadaint seis term,
uoss'ed adüna, seis linguach dal cour—
Rumantschs, dat pro!—Spendrai tras voss'amur
nos linguach da la mort da Tamangur!

is like the ancient forest gradually being ruined.
If the Rhaetians don't do their duty,
what happened to the forest will happen to them—Tamangur.

How could we forget that, since time immemorial,
the forest had guided our forebears?
A heritage they knew to prize and honor.
What shame it would bring, were we to let it fall.
Let's stand for what is ours, as others do for theirs,
and remember the end of Tamangur.

And no surrender!—Let no one forcefully take
from the Rhaetians their clearest right,
which is: to maintain, in their region,
today and always, the language of their heart—
Come, Rhaetians!—With your love
protect our language from the death of Tamangur.

ALEXANDER LOZZA

RETURN

La tgesa era tgoda scu en nia,
curtg'el bargiond ò detg adia.
Blers onns passos!—Igls vigls èn ve tar Dia.

El turna. Trest return! 'Gl'è tot schi freid!
Parfign an steiva, freid e veid.
Strousch cratschla l'oura viglia en saleid!

En ester, tranter esters stat el co!
Freids fardagliungs on detg: Ist no?
Scu egn tgi ò fallo cutier—el vo . . .

Angal la mamma or d'smiria portret
muaint' igls lefs, less deir en pled;
cun trest' igleida suondla igl poret . . .

ALEXANDER LOZZA

RETURN

Back then, the day he left, in tears,
the house had been a nest, so warm, for years.
So long ago now!—Dead, his parents, dear.

He returns. A sad return! So cold!
Objects seem strange—in the parlor, even—old.
The wall clock, alone, greets him. No fond hello—

He waits. As if not known here, he knows.
As if: the wrong house. What brings you so?
His siblings ask. And once again, he goes . . .

Only his mother's photo, paled in part,
seems to yearn for words; a heart to heart.
Her sad eyes watching as her son departs . . .

ARTUR CAFLISCH

IL ZURPLIN

Cur ch'impiz ün zurplin
am impais mincha geda
el es scu l'amur
üna flamma zuppeda.

E güst scu tar l'amur
eir tar el s'manifesta
cha sch'el clappa fö
schi and perda'l la testa.

IN ÜNA PINTA

Tschanto a mia maisa
sto'l co a buocha taisa,
la fixa d'ün cuntin
mas-chand vi d'ün zurplin,
ed eu am di, uzand ma fracla:
"Eir tü d'impizzast cun mincha s-chacla."

ARTUR CAFLISCH

THE MATCH

When I strike a match
I think every time
it is like love
a hidden flame.

And just as with love
it turns out
that by catching fire
it loses its head.

IN A TAVERN

He is sitting at my table
open-mouthed
ogling her
chewing a matchstick
and I say to myself, lifting my glass:
"You too will flare when struck on any box."

ENGLISH GLOSS BY THE EDITOR

VIC HENDRY

"ZACU INAGADA . . ."

zacu inagada
avon che jeu vomi
jeu less pertscheiver
ils radis che tremblan
osum la candeila
las larmas che neschan
caschunan legria
che bognan la crustas

"ANEMONA ALVA . . ."

anemona alva
creschas sin la tuma
arva tia casa
tegni la cazzola
freida ei la tiara
strusch pli da redember—
arva tia casa
anemona alva

VIC HENDRY

"JUST ONCE . . ."

just once
before I go
I'd like to grasp
the candle
its tip
those trembling rays

any welling tears
joyful
moisture
for the heart

"WHITE ANEMONE . . ."

white anemone
growing on the hill—

open up
and shine a light

the earth is cold
barely bearable

open up
white anemone

"GRISCHA E LONZIA . . ."

grischa e lonzia
in pugn mettadad
selai ca perreger
fitgada ell'urna
igl ei mo la tschendra

"GUILAS MELNAS CRODAN . . ."

guilas melnas crodan
sco'l sablun dall'ura
cusa la cusanza
il lenziel da bara
spetg'in tec cul tscherchel
ners igl ur che suonda
guilas melnas crodan

"TIRED GRAY HANDFUL . . ."

tired gray handful
of silence

no going back

committed to the urn

nothing but ash

"YELLOW NEEDLES FALLING . . ."

yellow needles falling
like sand in an hourglass

the seamstress sewing
the shroud still

hold off
with that black border

yellow needles
falling

ANDRI PEER

UCLAN

Las chasas scruoschan
aint il sulai da marz.
Il mezdi s'ha plachà
cun alas da sprer.

Il cheu pozzà cunter il mür,
vezza tras larmas
a passar speravia
l'uffant ch'eu d'eira.

TEJA BANDUNADA

La genna sgrigna
suot las scundunadas
dal vent.
La pensla sguotta
secundas planas.

Flöchs da naiv
aint ils zaps dal muvel.
Las muos-chas sun persas.

Che scruoscha quaint,
cur cha tü coccast
sün porta?

ANDRI PEER

A HAMLET

The houses crackle
in the March sun.
Noon has swooshed down
with the wings of a buzzard.

I rest my head against the wall
and through tears
see a child pass,
the child I once was.

MOUNTAIN HUT, ABANDONED

The fence groans
as the wind
elbows it.
From the eaves,
time falls wearily.

Snowflakes
in the cattle tracks.
The flies stray, lost.

What will creak
behind the door
if you knock?

DUMENGIA IN CHAMPOGNA

Omagi a Albin Zollinger

Ün orgel da man
chi largia il scuffel,
il dschem d'üna genna
ed ün rafüdar da sains.
Il sulai savura da ziplas
e'l vent ha peis da puolvra.

Il culaischem ais pardert
fingià d'üna pezza,
ils giodens süan largià.

Our'in vamporta tschaintan ils vegls
e fouran cul bastun illa glera,
tendan lur fatschas spassidas
sü vers la glüm.

Üerlidas da tromba
as sclavezzan
sülla chantunada,
s-charpan il quaid da l'ura.
Aint in üert d'ustaria
ramplunan maisas.
Ils tuns da schluppet dan giaischliadas
sur il gran madür.

SUNDAY IN THE COUNTRY

In memory of Albin Zollinger

The accordion,
and laughter
takes to its feet,
garden gates creak,
the bells fade.
The smell of sun in the sawdust
the wind's dusty feet.

The rowan has been waiting
a fair while already.
The attics are sweating resin.

Old people,
raking the gravel
out the front,
turn their withered faces
to the light.

Toots of horns
rupture the silence.
The beer garden
rattles.
Shots whip
over the ripe corn.

TAGLIALAINA

Tanter zuondra e bruoch
n'haja tendü meis talèr.
Vusch da resgia e sgür,
chantins da la daman.

Il dschember sbrajazza
seis pail verd.
Las nuschpignas sun glüms
da blaua aspettativa.

FURNATSCH

Amo scha tü sast tadlar
Resuna la bocca dal grip
D'üna vusch be suldüm
Chi nasch'illa not d'avuost
Aivra da fains muantats
E sflatschöz da forellas

Ella crescha aint il cuvel
Cull'odur da föglia d'serp
E d'erba schmaladida
Serpagiond in stiglia spirala
Ün füm d'insainas—
Povra vusch cuntriada
Chi's sduvl'our dal verd
Ed alvainta illa fanzögna
Da sias döglias vardaivlas
Chalischs da fö

THE WOODCUTTER

Between mugo pines and erica
I've plied my trade.
In the morning, the saw,
the ax, their vocals.

The swiss pine
bristles its green hair.
Its cones, lights
of blue expectation.

FURNATSCH

Listen, if you're able, carefully,
and hear in the rock
a voice of solitude
born of this August night
drunk on the hay in the breeze
and the trout jumping

It grows in the cave
with its scent of bracken
and Iceland moss,
the smoke, its delicate spirals,
an oracle, coiling.
A poor helpless voice
freeing itself from the green,
raising in the trance
of its veritable woes
fiery chalices

Sibilla retica Silvana
Chürast suot marva dainta
La palantada tschimainta
Da tias s-chürdüms
O Furnatsch saduol d'offertas
Da che taimpel offais
Membra schlisürada?

Sün quaders vout e paraid
L'En tira la resgia
Ed aint il vöd chi suosda
Rimbomba sia chanzun
Da mürader e marangun
Cullas gïas da sablun
E cul bass da l'auazun
Tadlai tadlai tadlai
Che lavurader ch'eu sun

Larschs
Sül ur dal grip
Delireschan d'oracul
Stendan stendan aval
Lur bratscha chandalera
Tadlond il plont
Da las pelegrinas
Chi vegnan e van
E mâ nu stan
Curraintas s-chümaintas
Suot il sindal
Da lur verd coral

Silvana, Rhaetian *Sibylle*,
your numb fingers nurse
the smoldering legend
of your darknesses.
O Furnatsch, weary of offerings,
from which desecrated temple
these scattered limbs?

To the ashlars, vault and walls
the Inn takes its saw,
from the yawning void
echoes its song—
that of the bricklayer,
the carpenter—
its sand violins
and high-water bass,
hark hark hark—hear
what a crafter I am!

Larches
at the edge of the rock
shudder at the prophecy.
Lower their
candelabra arms,
and listen to the laments
of the pilgrims,
the women coming and going
never stopping
flowing foaming
beneath the veil
of their green chorales.

Il vent am stumpla
Sül pass eu sguond
Ils spazis fladan
Ün sen profuond
Che dieu am tschercha?
Eu'm sgrisch eu stun
E lasch mi'uraglia
Sül ümid sablun
Quel rumurar
Fin oura pro'l mar
Somber schomber
Da l'En chi passa
E mâ nu's lassa

Straglüschidas stilettan
La not da meis ögl
Meis cour rafüda da batter
Mi'orma nüda
Tanter las rivas
Sablunivas
Immez sbodats
Cluchers da las
Sumbrivas

The wind pushes me
The edge, I follow.
The spaces breathe
profound sense.
Which god is seeking me?
I shrink back, stop,
put my ear
to the damp sand
That roar
all the way to the sea
the dark drumming
of the Inn flowing
tirelessly flowing past

Summer lightning lights
my eyes' night
My heart ceases to beat
My soul lies naked
between the banks
the sandy banks
amid the ruins of belfries
the shadows

HENDRI SPESCHA

"GIA VAN ILS VENTS . . ."

Gia van ils vents da ventschida
a riva

Orvas sesarvan el grisch

Il di retegn aunc in radi
per la flur dalla glisch

RACCOLTA

Igl abandun
ei seplaccaus
sin miu schui

Utschala fuostga
dalla
notg

Neu dil grischverd
savonzan ils garlogns
per far raccolta

HENDRI SPESCHA

"THE EVENING BREEZES . . ."

The evening breezes
Arriving already

Gaps open up in the gray

The day holds back a ray
for the flower of light

HARVEST

Solitude
has settled
on my shoulder

Ash-gray
bird
nocturnal

From the grayish-green
woodlice emerge
to bring the harvest in

"USS . . ."

Uss tuornan
ils ners
dil tscheiver grond

Mauns da rascha
Fatschas alvaunas
Buccas da fiug

Uss miera
la spronza

LAVUR ENTIRA

Ti has rut mia bratscha
culs pals da disfidonza

Ti has sfundrau mei
el foss digl abandun

Ti has surtratg mei
cullas reits da beffa

Ti has fatg lavur entira

Mo mias plagas contan

"NOW . . ."

They're heading back now,
the black figures
of Carnival

Blackened hands
whitish faces
fiery red mouths

Hope, now,
is dying

A GOOD JOB

You've broken my arms
with the clubs of mistrust

You've lowered me into
the ditch of desolation

You've trapped me
in the nets of scorn

You've done a good job

My sores, though, are singing

"JEU HAI . . ."

Jeu hai mo ina lieunga
il silenzi

Jeu hai mo in possess
la paupradad

Jeu hai in mund entir

"EI NEIVA INA NEIV . . ."

Ei neiva ina neiv
e mia stiva ei odur da giazint

Ei neiva ina notg
e miu intern passadetgna

Ei neiva ina neiv en mei
e mias uras crodan
els lenzeuls
digl avegnir

"I HAVE . . ."

I have only one tongue
silence

I have only one possession
poverty

I have an entire world

"IT IS SNOWING A SNOW . . ."

It is snowing a snow
and my parlor is the sweet smell of hyacinth

It is snowing a night
and my innards are melancholy

It is snowing a snow within me
and my hours are falling
into the thin linen
of the future.

LUISA FAMOS

IL RUDÈ

Batterdögls
Sco serpaischems
Chi schmütschan
Laschond insajar
Fin giò'l fuond
Nossa vita

Sco ün fluid
Van tremblond
Tras e tras

Batterdögls
Voss cumgiats
Sun asprezza

Il revair
Rasain
D'ajer viv.

GONDA

Tuots sun passats . . .

Mô cur chi vain la prümavaira
Cur chi vain la stà
Cur chi vain l'utuon

LUISA FAMOS

RONDE

Moments
—fleeting
lizardlike—
bid us
savor
life to the full

flow
tremble
through us

Moments,
your parting
is bitter

The return
brimful
of air,
vivid.

GONDA

Everyone's gone . . .

But when spring comes
And when summer comes
And when autumn comes

E cur chi vain l'unviern
Dvaintan nouvas tias müraglias

Aint illa flur dals alossers
Aint illa crappa s-chodada dal sulai
Aint illa föglia gelgua dal baduogn
In la naivera e glatschera
Giran lur spierts
In erramaint
Cregns d'increschantüm . . .

Tuots sun passats.

PLÖVGIA

I pluova . . .
I pluova prümavaira

Chanzun incuntschainta
Sdaisd'increschantüm
Plövgia mütta
Perche tavellast
Darschainta
Tuotta tristezza
Lia cun tschierchels
Ils temps e
Las algordanzas
Mô tascha
Sco'l baduogn
Chi spetta
Sainza föglia
Sainza gniou

And when winter comes
New life comes into your ruins

In the cherry blossom
In the rock, warm in the sun
In the yellowing leaves of the birch
In the snow and the ice
Their ghosts
Wander, homesick . . .

Everyone's gone.

RAIN

It's raining . . .
It's raining spring.

Your unfamiliar song
makes me homesick

Mute rain,
what are you saying?

Remove the sadness,
all of it

Put bands on
times
and memories

But be as silent
as the birch

Il plouva adün'amo . . .
Plövgia da prümavaira.

LÜGL A RAMOSCH

Trais randulinas
Battan lur alas
Vi dal tschêl d'instà

Minchatant tremblan
Trais sumbrivas
Sülla fatschad'alba
Da ma chà.

L'ANGUEL CULLAS ALAS D'OR

Sül far not
Chamin'a l'ur dal tschêl
L'anguel cullas alas d'or
Davant las stailas via

Taidla'm
Stenda teis man
Be ün mumaint
Vers mia stüva
Tuot il far mal pigl'üna fin
Spetta
Anguel cullas alas d'or.

as it awaits
its first leaf
first nest

It's raining still . . .
Spring rain

JULY IN RAMOSCH

Three swallows
sweeping across
the summer sky

The quivering sometimes
of three shadows
across my house
its white façade.

THE ANGEL WITH THE GOLDEN WINGS

As night falls
he walks along the sky
and past the stars
—the angel with the golden wings.

Listen to me
Reach over
just a moment
to my snug berth
All suffering must end
Wait
Angel with the golden wings

LETA SEMADENI

BES-CHAS

Adüna darcheu
aintran
luotin
bes-chas
aint in meis destin

Üna vuolp vain
intuorn la chantunada
strond cun sai
ün chavà
ed ün prà

Eu lasch ir la stà
suravi ils cunfins

Inavrià
discuorra il chavà
ma favella

La vuolp
es aint ils latschs
da tantas istorgias

LETA SEMADENI

ANIMALS

Again
and again
an animal
slinks
through my texts

A fox comes
round the corner,
in its tow
a horse
and a meadow

I have the summer
drift over any borders

Intoxicated
the horse speaks
my language

The fox
intricated
in so many stories

DAVANT IL SERRAGL DALS CHUCALS

Al chucal
es l'uman
vacha chavà o chavra

La bes-cha
davant il serragl
nu sa nüglia
da la finezza dal gruogn
da la magia
cur cha saidla
as pozza sün saidla

AT THE PIG PEN

To pigs
humans are
cows goats or horses

The creatures
at the pen
know nothing
of the delicateness
of a snout
of the magic of bristle
meeting bristle

CLO DURI BEZZOLA

LIMITÀ

En il rom da mia fanestra
stattan trais lareschs
senza tschimas
e ragischs

Per vesair la tschima
ma stossa sgobar

Per dar egl las ragischs
ma stuessa dauzar

Uschia èsi pisserà
che la bostga
na creschia
fin en tschiel

CLO DURI BEZZOLA

LIMITED

In the window frame
three larches
with no crowns
no roots

To see the crowns
I have to bend down

For a glance at the roots
I'd have to stand up

Thus is ensured
the trees
won't grow
up into the sky

GÖRI KLAINGUTI

EXPERIMAINT CUN MOLEKÜLS DA H_2O

Fo ün fö cun flamma bella
metta sü üna sadella
cun aint üna pruna d'glatsch
suravi ün vierchelatsch.
Que sbarbuoglia e sfuschigna
misteriusa canerigna.
Già a qualche molekül
vain que chod suotaint il chül.

Ün as stordscha, l'oter schmacha
ed ün terz bod as distacha.
Auncha sune dieu ludo,
societed da H_2O.

Uossa fügian bgers in prescha
our dal chod chi penetrescha
ed els saglian vi e pü
impazchaints tres l'ova sü.

Al bun vierchel vain la pizcha
fin ch'el evr'üna sfalizcha
per lascher saglir ils tips
our il liber scu silips.
Quels as giodan e giuvaintan
svouls fantastics as invaintan
a festagian plain paschiun
taunta emanzipaziun.

GÖRI KLAINGUTI

EXPERIMENT WITH H$_2$O MOLECULES

Make a fire, nice and hot
over it, now place a pot
next, shake some ice in—go for it!
—then put the lid on, wait a bit.
The pot's soon rumbling, crackling, groaning,
hissing, spitting, popping, moaning,
the molecules, rapidly, in a tizzy,
short of breath, feeling dizzy.

Firmly trapped within the pot,
beneath their butts it's getting hot,
and yet, God knows, they're not morose,
this new-formed club of H$_2$Os.

They try to flee, now in a hurry,
as from the heat they seek to scurry.
Danger! Chaos!—and flaming heck:
disaster strikes—a bottleneck.

Poor lid! Behold, now, how it's rattling,
shaking, trembling, itching, battling
to keep these wee guys in. Out they get, though,
into freedom, fly this way, that way, so
elated—their flight paths know no bounds.
The escapees whiz, just, round and round.
Emancipation, they seem to call,
is a cause for joy to one and all.

Uossa tegnast, fand cuaida,
üna granda lastra fraida
ot sur els davent dal fö.
Tuots s'allegran dal bel lö.
Inguordatschs insü as büttan
e pel melder lö's dispüttan.
Ma apaina arrivos
vezzast svelt cha sun schocos.

Üna vampa da fradaglia
a minchün dad els assaglia,
faun la pêsch pü cu gugent
per surviver il spavent.
A decidan lur instanzas
da s'unir in radunanzas
e furmer da tuots per tuots
üna societed da guots.

Ma la lastra es suot nolla,
ils fantasts sun suot controlla
ed els stöglian ster cun s-chif
ün sper l'oter bel guliv.
Uoss'es dschiett'e melcuntainta
tuotta molekülamainta
ma ün uorden exempler
darcho regna traunter pêr.

It's time to reach now for a plate
and watch the fun that you create
if you hold it high above your head,
close to the pot (take that as read).
A mad, mad rush is next, for sure.
What you witness next is chaos pure
as the plate is raced toward, so erratically,
you can't account for it, mathematically.

A shock is next. The shock of the cold
hits every molecule, however bold.
Now watch this one, that one, as—indeed—
they turn to friends in time of need.
Associations are quickly formed,
solidarity suddenly the norm,
a unanimous vote, at the end of their tether,
for *side by side*, for coming-together.

It's sub-zero, though, this plate
—rendering meaningless any debate.
It's time for all these molecules
quite simply, now, to follow rules,
and however high emotions ride,
to concede and lie down, side by side.

And though, moments before, things on mutiny bordered,
The new theme is *brotherly*. At the same time, *ordered*.

RUT PLOUDA

NOTS

I dà nots
chi's plajan intuorn las spadlas
sco saida,
i dà nots
chi spettan coura
sco ladras,
nots
sco tailas d'arogn
tanter fögliom e früts cotschens
e nots
chi'ns piglian adascus
e'ns transmüdan.

DAVANT IL SPEJEL

Eu m'ha guardada
in fatscha
il temp fa pajaglia
eu vegn a pè scuz
tras meis god inchantà

ant co tuornar
zopparaja meis sömmis
suot müs-chel brünaint

RUT PLOUDA

NIGHTS

There are nights
that, like silk, go
around your shoulders.

Nights
that loiter
like a thief, outside.

Nights
like cobwebs
between the fruit and the foliage

And nights
that steal up
and transform us.

BEFORE THE MIRROR

In my face
traces of time
smile at me

I walk barefoot
through my enchanted forest

but before heading home
hide my dreams
under brownish moss

"I NAIVENAIVENAIVA . . ."

I naivenaivenaiva
mütta
la scenaria
be vuolp ria
stigl
ün sigl
la vita
es hoz sia

"IT SNOWSANDSNOWSANDSNOWS . . ."

It snowsandsnowsandsnows
silent
scenery

Only the fox
sniggers to himself
leaps

Life
is his,
today

DUMENIC ANDRY

TIRADA E RETIRADA

Saimpel, totel, tamberlan,
Cacalar', mamau, salam,
Toc tschavat, schogn, zoch, schiloner,
Imbitschil, minchun, tschambocker,
Püf, bizoccal, maccarun,
Cuc, rambot e clavarun,
Mül, crabot, moccus, stival,
Tü chanaster, animal,
Rost, chajot, strüzzel, macac,
Tau, raduond, pluffer, margnac,
Toc implaster, cot a dür,
Tü martuffel e cheudür,
Tü tamberl, tü tais, tambur,
Toc tschigrun toc da la guotta,
Valanöglia ed inguotta,
Toc armaint, toc tabalori,
Tü merder e salvanori,
Tü chastör, schmachapuglinas,
Tü daschüttel, stranglagiallinas,
Maladester e maslvout,
Ah tü asen o schumar . . .

Uossa prada't, est bain nar,
Da vulair s-chargiar sün mai,
D'quists sgradaivels sinonims
Grond mantun, pover tagnin,
Tegna pür ün pêr per tai!

DUMENIC ANDRY

A RANT & A RESPONSE

Ya cuntin fuckin bastard ye.
Ya asshole, fuckin asshole.
Naw: keep your crap, shite, fuckin shite
to yourself. Think I'm fuckin—Naw: where the—
Why the—*How* the fuck did ye—
Do ye think I'm fuckin thick or what,
ya dickhead. Naw: get to fuck, piss off, ya dick,
fuck off just—shaft some other cunt, ya dick.
Don't fuckin go trying fuckin to fuckin shaft me,
ya cunt, don't come the bastarn cunt with me,
out of order, that's what you fuckin are, fuckin
out of order, fuckin out of order ye were, and don't go
fuckin trying fuckin to fuckin deny it either, ya dick ye,
ya bastard ye, ya total fuckin cunt ye, fuckin
dickhead, prick so you are—

What's your *point*, mate? Spit it out!
It's not like ye to mince your words.
Forget the verbal diarrhea for a mo.
Get a grip. Face facts. Look at yourself
for once, ya big shite. Ya poor sod.
Think "kettle." Think "calling." Think "pot black"!

(FREELY ADAPTED)

245

ARNO CAMENISCH

"IL TAT HA INA VACCA . . ."

il tat ha ina vacca la tatta fa salata
il tat ha bugen la vacca la tatta ei granata
il tat ha si cassacca la tatta fa baracca
il tat ha bugen salata il gat silpli la gatta
la tatta ha bugen il tat igl auto mellen lez ha plat
la tatta ha bugen il tat igl auto mellen ha plaz per siat
il tat lez vul far fiasta la tatta dat cull'asta
il tat lez ei granata la tatta di el batta
la tatta vendi'il gat il tat fa star la gatta
la tatta vend'il tat il tat di so uss basta

"NEGIN CHE CAPESCHA . . ."

Negin che capescha tgei ch'el di Negin che
capescha tgei ch'el ha da dir Jeu sai dir
tgei ch'jeu vi mais qu'est-ce qu'il a dit?
El sa di tgei ch'ei bi El sa di tgei ch'ei da
dir Was isch jetz gsi? Je crois qu'il a dit
qu'il n'a rien dit Ed in bi di eis el da leuvi
ed aunc adina negin che sa tgei ch'el
leva propi dir quei bi di negin che sa tgei
ch'el haveva da dir quei bi di si a Helsinki

ARNO CAMENISCH

"GRANDPA HAS A LLAMA..."

grandpa has a llama grandma's fixing salad
grandpa likes his llama grandma's getting mad-mad
grandpa in his balaclava grandma drinking going gaga
grandpa likes his salad grandma sings a ballad
grandma likes her ballad grandpa's looking pallid
grandma likes ma grandpa he'd prefer a panda
grandpa wants to party grandma calls him smarty
grandpa's getting mad-mad grandma says he's gaga
grandma sells the llama grandpa gets a panda
grandma sells ma grandpa grandpa swears he'll tell ma ma

(FREELY ADAPTED)

"YOU CAN'T MAKE OUT A WORD THE GUY SAYS..."

You can't make out a word the guy says. Can't begin
to understand what he's trying to say. Me, I can
say what I want, ay. Rothesay, he's frae.* Yes, Rothesay.
Oh aye, he knows what *they* want to hear him say. Knows
what it is they'd *like* him to say. Qu'est-ce que c'est?
Sure, one fine day, he'll pass away. But even
that day, no one will know what he wanted to say.
Not a scooby,** as they say. Even in Rothesay.

(FREELY ADAPTED)

---

* A dialect form of "from."
** *Scooby*—from "Scooby Doo"—is rhyming slang for "clue."

"LA ZOPPA EI MORTA . . ."

La zoppa ei morta ei satiaran la zoppa
dei adatg culla comba di enzatgi
cu ei mettan la zoppa el vischi

"THE WOMAN WITH THE LIMP DIES . . ."

the woman with the limp dies, they bury the woman with the limp
watch her leg, some guy gives it
as they put her in the coffin, the woman with the limp

IV
GERMAN

TRANSLATED BY BURTON PIKE (BP)
AND REINHARD MAYER,
WITH THE ASSISTANCE OF
LAUREN K. WOLFE (RM),
SAVE WHERE INDICATED.

ROBERT WALSER

WEITER

Ich wollte stehen bleiben,
es trieb mich wieder weiter,
vorbei an schwarzen Bäumen,
doch unter schwarzen Bäumen
wollt' ich schnell stehen bleiben,
es trieb mich wieder weiter,
vorbei an grünen Wiesen,
doch an den grünen Wiesen
wollt' ich nur stehen bleiben,
es trieb mich wieder weiter,
vorbei an armen Häuschen,
bei einem dieser Häuschen
möcht' ich doch stehen bleiben,
betrachtend seine Armut,
und wie sein Rauch gemächlich
zum Himmel steigt, ich möchte
jetzt lange stehen bleiben.
Dies sagte ich und lachte,
das Grün der Wiesen lachte
der Rauch stieg räuchlich lächelnd,
es trieb mich wieder weiter.

ROBERT WALSER

ONWARDS

I wanted to stop,
it drove me on again,
past black trees,
yet under black trees
I wanted to stop for a bit,
it drove me on again,
past green meadows,
yet by the green meadows
I just wanted to stop,
it drove me on again,
past poor hovels,
at one of these hovels
I would like to stop,
observing its poverty,
and how its smoke
rises leisurely to the sky,
now I would like to stop for long.
I said this and laughed,
the green of the meadows laughed
the smoke rose smokily smiling,
it drove me on again.

BP

UND GING

Er schwenkte leise seinen Hut
und ging, heisst es vom Wandersmann.
Er riss die Blätter von dem Baum
und ging, heisst es vom rauhen Herbst.
Sie teilte lächelnd Gnaden aus
und ging, heisst's von der Majestät.
Es klopfte nächtlich an die Tür
und ging, heisst es vom Herzeleid.
Er zeigte weinend auf sein Herz
und ging, heisst es vom armen Mann.

BEISEIT

Ich mache meinen Gang;
der führt ein Stückchen weit
und heim; dann ohne Klang
und Wort bin ich beiseit.

AND WENT

He doffed his hat softly and went,
so it's said of the wayfaring man.
It stripped the trees of their leaves and went,
thus the austere autumn wind.
She doled out her mercies with a smile
and went on her royal way, the queen.
Night after night it knocked at the door
and it went away, this of a broken heart.
At his heart he pointed weeping and he went,
so it's said of the man who has naught.

RM

ASIDE

I take a walk; it takes
me a bit far, a bit wide
and home; then without
sound or word, alone,
it's myself I'm beside.

RM

COUPLET

Ich bin mir schuldig, dass ich nächstdem lese einen Band von
  Marcel Proust
bis heut' ist mir noch nicht das Mindeste von diesem eminenten
  Mann bewusst.

Vom Fuggerhaus zu Augsburg fand ich kürzlich ein'ge Zeitschrift-
  abbildungen
und bin an Hand derselben in den Handelsblütezustand Deutsch-
  lands eingedrungen.

Den Stuhl, von dem ein Fräulein sich erhoben hatte, sah ich euch,
  o Freunde, glänzen
vor nichts, als vor Vergnügtheit wegen Diensterwiesenheits-
  tendenzen.

In einer Kirche sang ein Sängerinnenexemplar so unbeschreiblich
  schön, ich will's gestehn,
dass ich mir erstens rein wie Schnee und andersteils erweicht
  erschien bis zum Zergehn.

Heut' früh erhielt ich einen vor Gekränktheit fassungslosen,
  tiefergriffnen Brief.
Auf Grund des Inhalts, der mich nicht beruhigt lassen sollte,
  schlief ich tief.

Noch hat der Zwiespalt zwischen Lebenswunsch und Schaffens-
  drang mich nie gar lang belästigt,
Natur und ein Glas Wein in einem Landgasthaus haben mich
  jeweils hübsch in mir befestigt.

COUPLET

I'm shamefully remiss in not having read a single volume of Marcel
   Proust;
to this day I don't know the least bit of what this eminent man's
   produced.

I came across a few illustrations of the Augsburg Fugger Houses
   in a magazine somewhere
and on account of these was overcome by the flourishing state of
   German commercial affairs.

The chair that a girl just stood up from, I saw it, oh friends,
   practically rapturous
for no other reason than the pleasure it takes in its inherent
   tendency to render service.

In a church I heard a singer singing, so unutterably lovely it was I
   feel I have to confess
I felt at first stark and pure as newfallen snow, then suddenly
   softened, as if I'd evanesce.

I received a bewildering letter this morning, the author of which
   was profoundly aggrieved.
On the strength of its content, not intended to appease, I fell
   prompt and deeply asleep.

The tension between life's desires and the creative urge has seldom
   inconvenienced me;
nature and a glass of wine at a rural inn have been enough to
   steady me in myself rather nicely.

Tolstoi starb aus Verdruss, dass ihm das Leben, das er liebte, nicht
   mehr schmeckte;
ein Dichterfürst wie Shakespeare ihn mit seiner klaren Tragik,
   trocknen Komik neckte.

O, von welch blühender Unsterblichkeit ist wieder dieser doch so
   unkomplett gewesne Heinrich Heine.
Frau Mitwelt hielt ihm vor, er sei nicht sauber, doch die Dame
   Nachwelt kam mit ihm ins Reine.

Tolstoy died of his displeasure that the life he loved he no longer
savored;
for him, the bold tragedy, the dry comedy of a poet-prince like
Shakespeare rancored.

Oh, the florid immortality of Heinrich Heine, the man had indeed
so incompletely been.
While Miss Social Life reproached him, called him corrupted,
with Lady Afterlife he came clean.

RM

REGINA ULLMANN

IM MOHNFELD ZUR GEWITTERSZEIT

Ich ging im Mohnfeld zur Gewitterszeit
vor vielen Jahren—
und es war mein Kleid
von rotem Seidenstoff und mächtig weit . . .
wie umgestülpter Mohn aus Seidenhaaren.

Und schlug ein Rad aus mir und deckt' das Feld
vor den Gefahren—
und rief als Zeugen mich der höhern Welt,
die mich auf dieses rote Feld bestellt
für diesen Tag vor ungezählten Jahren!

"UND STIRBT SIE AUCH . . ."

Und stirbt sie auch,
so trifft dich kein Verschulden.
Sie hat sich ihren Tod
selbst wie ein Hemd gewoben
und hat sich eng und hart hineingeschoben,
die Formeln murmelnd,
die diesen grauen Sinn
nach innen wachsen machen
und sie ganz umschliessen.
Dass nicht ein Baum
und nicht ein Vogelsang
und alle Süsse, die in reifen Früchten
geborgen ist,

REGINA ULLMANN

IN A POPPY FIELD IN THE MIDDLE OF A STORM

I wandered in a poppy field in the middle of a storm
years ago it must have been—
and it was my dress,
wide hemmed and woven of red silk thread . . .
like a silken poppy, inverted, billowing in the wind.

And I turned a cartwheel, was overturned, and covered the field
from danger, from wind—
a higher world had called me as witness, it was as if
I had been appointed: me, to this red field, to this very day
untold years ago, it must have been!

"AND SHOULD SHE DIE . . ."

And should she die,
you shall not meet with debt.
She has woven her death
herself like a shirt
and eased herself inside, tight and firm,
murmuring the formulae
that cause the dread sense
to grow, inwardly
and to encase her.
So that no tree
nor birdsong, nothing
of the sweetness that ripe fruit
encloses within it

sie jemals mehr durchbricht.
Sie stirbt so wie ein Stein
in sandiger Ebene.
Es wird ihn keiner finden,
dies Sein zerteilt sich wieder
in das Land.
Und nur Jahrtausende noch,
die verwandeln
im Kreisen ihrer Erde,
sagen riesig: lieben.

LEBENDES BILD

Erwartungsvoll harren die Vielfachzerstreuten
eng aneinandergedrückt, Schulter an Schulter,
auf das lebendig gesammelte Spiel.
Aber wie sich der Vorhang hinauftut,
ist es mehr, als ihre Herzen zu fassen vermögen,
ist es eines der Wunder des Überflusses,
wie sie der Heiland im Fischfang getan
oder in der Mehrung der Brote.
Und sie schauen wie die Fischer
nach dem Ufer des Schauspiels,
dass jene ihnen helfen,
das Netz ins Schiff ziehn . . .
und sie tragen mit den Jüngern des Herrn,
was übriggeblieben, zwölf Körbe an Brocken,
hinweg,
erfasst von der grossen Geste des Mitleids.

Dann lehnen sie wieder sich an das Gegenwärtige an
wie Mutter Maria an ihren Sohn, den Johannes

will ever break through that encasement again.
She dies thus like a stone
in a sandy plain,
which no one will find,
its being abraded
again into land.
And only the centuries,
turning in circles,
transforming their earth,
vastly they say: love.

TABLEAU VIVANT

Expectantly the manifold scattered now wait,
pressed close, one on another, shoulder to shoulder,
for the collective living drama to unfold.
Though when the curtain is lifted
it is more than their hearts can fathom,
it is a drama of miracles of abundance,
such as the Savior performed by fishing
or in the multiplication of loaves.
And they look, like the fishermen,
over toward the drama's shores,
as if this might help the men
haul their nets aboard . . .
and they bear, with the Son of God,
all that remained, twelve baskets with fragments of bread,
away,
gripped by the extravagant gesture of mercy.

Then they lean again into their contemporaries,
like Mary leaning against her son John,

und sinken mit der blassen
aschblonden Magdalena über der Narde zusammen,
als sei sie der Herr selbst,
und senken ihn weinend
mit letzten Kräften ins Grab,
die dreifach gelittne Passion beerdigend.

Leise rollt der Vorhang darüber sich aus,
doch erlischt nicht darunter das Bild:
denn wirklicher als eine Blume
je darin sein kann oder ein Vogel
und Duft und Farbe
und schwankende Windesbewegung,
ist eines Menschenherzens
wiederklingendes Leid.

and they swoon like the pale
blonde Magdalena swoons over spikenard,
as if she were herself the Lord,
and they lower him weeping
with the last of their strength into the grave,
interring the thrice-suffered passion.

Slowly the curtain closes upon it,
yet the scene is not extinguished:
for more real than any flower
that features in it, or bird
and fragrance and color
and the wavering wind can ever be,
is the resounding sorrow
of the human heart.

                                                        RM

EMMY BALL-HENNINGS

KLEINE GASSE AM ABEND

Bunte Mädchen lugen aus schmalen Fenstern
Der Mond wirft geisterhaftes Licht.
Aus blauen Schatten ragt grelles Gesicht
In der Gasse wimmelt es von Gespenstern.

Ein Droschkenkutscher hält sein Pferd umschlungen
Die himmelhohe Liebe rauscht im Blut.
Und Rosen verkauft die kleine Rut.
"Zu Mantua in Banden" wird gesungen.

Oh, das Klavier tut, was es kann.
Gewiss, man spielt nicht schön, doch laut.
Ein Schlafbursche umarmt eine fremde Braut
Schwört ewige Treue, so dann und wann . . .

EMMY BALL-HENNINGS

NARROW LANE AT NIGHT

Painted girls peek from the windows
The moon casts a spectral light.
From blue shadows a lurid sight looms
The narrow lane is teeming with ghosts.

A cabdriver has his horse by the reins
Love courses ardent in the veins.
And little Ruth is out peddling roses.
The Andreas-Hofer-Lied's being sung.

Oh, the piano does what it can.
Of course the player's no good though he's loud.
A boarder embraces a foreign bride
So that when and if . . . faith eternal's avowed

RM

HUGO BALL

CABARET

1.

Der Exhibitionist stellt sich gespreizt am Vorhang auf
und Pimpronella reizt ihn mit den roten Unterröcken.
Koko der grüne Gott klatscht laut im Publikum.
Da werden geil die ältesten Sündenböcke.

Tsingtara! Da ist ein langes Blasinstrument.
Daraus fährt eine Speichelfahne. Darauf steht: "Schlange".
Da packen alle ihre Damen in die Geigenkästen ein
und verziehen sich. Da wird ihnen bange.

Am Eingang sitzt die ölige Camödine.
Die schlägt sich die Goldstücke als Flitter in die Schenkel.
Der sticht einer Bogenlampe die Augen aus.
Und das brennende Dach fällt herunter auf ihren Enkel.

HUGO BALL

CABARET

1.

The exhibitionist splays himself next to the curtain.
And Pimpronella teases him with her pink petticoats.
In the audience Koko the Green God is rowdy and
clapping and lusty grow the hoary old goats.

Tsingtara! There is a long brass instrument. From it
dangles a spittle pennant on which it is written: Serpent.
Now everyone stows their ladies in violin cases
and excuses themselves. Anxiety is coming unpent.

At the entrance the slick Camödine is seated,
slapping coins like sequins against her thighs.
An arc lamp is gouging out her eyes.
And the burning roof falls upon her grandchild.

2.

Von dem gespitzten Ohr des Esels fängt die Fliegen
ein Clown, der eine andre Heimat hat.
Durch kleine Röhrchen, die sich grünlich biegen,
hat er Verbindung mit Baronen in der Stadt.

In hohen Luftgeleisen, wo sich enharmonisch
die Seile schneiden, drauf man flach entschwirrt,
Versucht ein kleinkalibriges Kamel platonisch
zu klettern; was die Fröhlichkeit verwirrt.

Der Exhibitionist, der je zuvor den Vorhang
bedient hat mit Geduld und Blick für das Douceur,
vergisst urplötzlich den Begebenheitenvorgang
und treibt gequollene Mädchenscharen vor sich her.

2.

From the pointed ear of an ass a clown
catches flies. He's not from around here.
He has slender tubes that bend viridescent
that connect him with the barons in town.

High wires intersect the air enharmonically
in lofted tracks where a man whirls away flat
and a small-calibered camel platonically attempts
his own ascent; the general mirth is confused by that.

The exhibitionist who heretofore has tended
the curtain with patience and an eye out for tips
suddenly forgets the sequence of events
and drives gushing multitudes of girls *en avance*.

RM

"WEH UNSER GUTER KASPAR IST TOT . . ."

weh unser guter kaspar ist tot.
wer trägt nun die brennende fahne im zopf. wer dreht die kaffeemühle. wer lockt das idyllische reh.
auf dem meer verwirrte er die schiffe mit dem wörtchen parapluie und die winde nannte er bienenvater.
weh weh weh unser guter kaspar ist tot. heiliger bimbam kaspar ist tot.
die heufische klappern in den glocken wenn man seinen vornamen ausspricht darum seufze ich weiter kaspar kaspar kaspar.
warum bist du ein stern geworden oder eine kette aus wasser an einem heissen wirbelwind oder ein euter aus schwarzem licht oder ein durchsichtiger ziegel an der stöhnenden trommel des felsigen wesens.
jetzt vertrocknen unsere scheitel und sohlen und die feen liegen halbverkohlt auf den scheiterhaufen. jetzt donnert hinter der sonne die schwarze kegelbahn und keiner zieht mehr die kompasse und die räder der schiebkarren auf.
wer isst nun mit der ratte am einsamen tisch. wer verjagt den teufel wenn er die pferde verführen will. wer erklärt uns die monogramme in den sternen.
seine büste wird die kamine aller wahrhaft edlen menschen zieren doch das ist kein trost und schnupftaback für einen totenkopf.

HANS ARP

"WOE OUR GOOD KASPAR IS DEAD . . ."

woe our good kaspar is dead.
now who will wear the burning banner in his hair. who work
the coffee grinder. who entice the idyllic roebuck.
at sea he confused the ships with the little word umbrella and
called the winds beekeeper.
woe woe woe our good kaspar is dead. oh my saintly kaspar is
dead.
the sharks rattle in the bells when one utters his first name
that's why I keep sighing kaspar kaspar kaspar.
why have you become a star or a chain of water on a hot whirl-
wind or an udder of black light or a transparent brick on the
moaning drum of rocky being.
now our skulls and soles are drying out and the fairies lie half
charred burned at the stake. now behind the sun the black bowl-
ing alley thunders and no one winds up the compass and the
wheels of the wheelbarrow any longer.
who now eats with the rats at the lonely table. who chases away
the devil when he wants to make off with the horses. who ex-
plains to us the monograms in the stars.
his bust will adorn the mantelpieces of all truly noble people
but that is no comfort or snuff for a death's-head.

BP

ALBIN ZOLLINGER

SONNTAG

Ganz ferne Musik.
Mundharmonika oder Kirchweih.
Es riecht nach Sonne in Sägespänen.
Hemdärmel der Knechte
Bauschen sich, Bohnenblüten.
In Kammern tropft Harz.
Vom Sommer der Zeitung
Schlummert der Ahn
In bestaubten Kamillen.
Radfahrervereine
Läuten schalmeiend vorüber.
Der Biergarten klappert.

WO ABER FLIEGEN DIE ABENDVÖGEL HIN?

Die Tauben schlummern im Hause:
Wo aber fliegen die Abendvögel hin?
Der Wasserfall dämpft sein Gebrause:
Wo aber rinnen die Bäche hin?
Friedlich wurzelt der Rauch auf den Dächern:
Wo aber strömt das Nachtgewölk hin?
Lichter stehen in tausend Gemächern:
Wo aber sinken die Sterne hin?
Immer indem wir liegen und schlafen
Lösen sich Schiffe dunkel vom Hafen.

ALBIN ZOLLINGER

SUNDAY

Music in the distance.
A harmonica or a fair.
It smells like sun in the sawdust.
Workers' shirtsleeves
Billowing, bean blossoms.
In cabins resin drips.
The summer, the news
Has put the older generation to sleep
Among chamomiles
Covered in dust.
Bicycle clubs
Ring oboeing by.
The beer garden clanks.

WHERE DO THE EVENING BIRDS FLY?

Doves are slumbering in the dovecot:
But where do the evening birds fly?
The waterfall tamps its roar:
But where do the rivers run?
Smoke from chimneys lingers over rooftops:
But where do the winds drive the night clouds?
Lights shine in thousands of houses:
But where do the stars go to set?
Whilst we are lying down sleeping
Ships set sail darkly from harbors.

RM

ALBERT STREICH

UF STEINIGEM BODEN

Han i es chliins Liedelli gsungen.
Vom Wäärden, vom Siin und Vergahn,
es Väärsli i d Liit uusi bbrungen.
Die hei's due nid wiiters meh gsungen,
derwiil nid und ds Herz, 's es z verstahn.

Su liid's uf em steinigen Boden
im Steub und am Wätter, im Wind
Bis vlicht eis mit ubholffene Chnoden
näbenuus uf steinigem Boden
e Seel, e verschipfti, 's es findt.

ALBERT STREICH

ON STONY GROUND

I sang a small song.
Of becoming, of being and ceasing to be,
a particle of verse I gave to the people.
They sing it no more,
no time and no heart more have they to hear it.

So there it lies on the stony ground,
exposed, to dust and storm, to wind,
until some calloused and heavy hand
near to the stony ground,
a soul, one adrift, finds it.

INDUUCHLEN

Aabe chunnd
uber Bäärge embrin,
leid si im Grund
sametig hin.

Liid ubere Wääldern,
si gspirren ne chuumm,
liid ubere Fäldren
en duuchliga Flumm.

Spinnd um mi z ringsum
und liired mi in.
Weis niimma, ob i diheimmen
old wiit, wiit furt bin.

DARKENING

Evening comes
over the mountains
to set in the valley
softly, as velvet.

Coming to rest
over the forest
that can barely sense it,
over the downs,
softly as such.

It spins itself
and swaddles me.
I don't know anymore
if I'm at home
or far far from it.

RM

RAINER BRAMBACH

ALTERSHEIM

Als Gärtner im Ruhestand lebend,
kenne ich noch immer
den Fahrplan aller acht Winde.
Meine Prognosen,
wann das Regengewölk eintreffen wird,
sind verlässlich.

Ausser der Gicht und dem unstillbaren Gelüst
nach einem Glas Schnaps
plagt mich nichts. Meine Freunde sind tot
und die Feinde verschollen.

Diese Welt, die ich nicht mehr verstehe,
besucht mich in Gestalt einer Zeitung
jede Woche einmal,
und mehrmals täglich
schwirrt eine Schar von Spatzen ans Fenster.

Für erwiesenes Vertrauen habe ich sie
zum Buchfinken erhoben.

RAINER BRAMBACH

OLD FOLKS' HOME

A gardener once, retired now,
I remember still
the timetable for each of the eight cardinal winds.
My prognoses,
when the storm clouds roll in,
are reliable.

Apart from the gout and my insatiable desire
for a glass of schnapps,
nothing bothers me. My friends are dead
and my enemies forgotten.

This world, that I don't understand anymore,
calls on me in the guise of a newspaper,
once a week,
and several times a day
a host of sparrows flits past my window.

On the basis of the good faith they've shown me,
I've nominated them
chaffinches.

ALLEINSTEHENDE MÄNNER

Einer sammelt Steine.
Einer erwirbt Briefmarken.
Ein dritter spielt Fernschach
und einer steht lauernd am Abend im Park.
Einer lernt Russisch.
Einer liest Shakespeare.
Einer schreibt Brief um Brief
und einer trinkt Rotwein am Abend,
sonst geschieht nichts.
Sie trinken, lesen, lauern, erwerben,
die Männer allein am Abend.
Sie schreiben, lernen, spielen, sammeln,
ein jeder für sich nach Feierabend.
Einer besucht eine Operette.
Einer hört Bach.
Einer hütet ein Geheimnis.
Wie ein Hund an der Kette
läuft er Abend für Abend entlang der Alleen.

SINGLE MEN

One collects rocks,
one postage stamps.
A third plays correspondence chess,
and one lurks furtively at night in the park.
One's learning Russian.
One's reading Shakespeare.
One writes letter after letter,
while another drinks red wine each night.
Otherwise, nothing's going on.
They drink, read, lurk, shop,
all the men who're alone at night.
They write, study, play, collect,
each one for himself after work.
One attends an operetta.
One listens to Bach.
There's one who's keeping a secret
like a dog on a leash,
night after night he races up and down through the street.

RM

GERHARD MEIER

RONDO

Während über Manhattan
der Tag untergeht
wie er überm Dorf
untergeht
und es nach Wäldern riecht
nach Fliegen
verlorenen
Wegen

werden den Kühen
die Euter entleert

und morgen trinken
die Milch sie in Städten
während der Tag heraufkommt
wie ein Mime heraufkommt
sozusagen durch die Bretter
auf die Bretter kommt

werden den Kühen
die Euter entleert

und abends trinken
die Milch sie in Städten
während über Manhattan
der Tag untergeht
wie ein Mime von der
Bühne geht
und sich einer ans Fenster setzt
den Nachtwind zu spüren

GERHARD MEIER

RONDO

While over Manhattan
the day recedes
as over the village
it recedes
and smells of forests
of flies
lost
paths

the udders of cows
are emptied

and tomorrow those
in the cities
drink the milk
as the day rises
the way an actor appears
so to speak up from the boards,
treads the boards

the udders of cows
are emptied

and evenings milk is drunk
in the cities
while over Manhattan
the day recedes
like an actor who leaves the stage
and a person sits down by the window
to feel the night wind.

DANN WIEDER DIE AMSEL

Sah einen schmutzigen
Jungen
Mülltonne
um
Mülltonne
durchwühlen
in der Frühe der
Grossstadt—
und er pfiff

Sah ein mongoloides
Mädchen seine
Handtasche von
Huthaken
zu
Huthaken
hängen
während der Predigt—
und es strahlte

Sah ruhige Passanten
promenieren
sonntags beim
Einnachten
und frage mich
wie die es machen—

Dies Jahr wird's
Kirschen geben
kann's Kirschen
geben

THEN THE BLACKBIRD AGAIN

Saw a filthy
kid
pawing through
garbage bin
after
garbage bin
in the big city's dawn—
and he was whistling

Saw a mongoloid girl
hanging her purse
on hat peg after hat peg
during the sermon—
and she was radiant

Saw calm passersby
promenading Sundays
as night fell
and ask myself
how do they do it—

This year there'll
be cherries
can be cherries

An express train imposes
on the surroundings
its language

Then the blackbird again

Ein Schnellzug zwingt
der Umgebung seine
Sprache auf

Dann wieder die Amsel

DIE STRASSE LANG PFEIFT EINE AMSEL

Ostwind
beleckt die Strassen
Das Kopfsteinpflaster des Nadelöhrs
ist feucht 's wird Regen
geben

Steinhauer
stellen Steine zur Schau
Haarschneider wischen Haare zuhauf
Kommentatoren verloren den
Hasen

Inzwischen
hat der Wind gedreht
Die Strasse lang pfeift eine
Amsel

ALONG THE STREET A BLACKBIRD SINGS

East wind
licks at the streets
the cobbled pavement at the narrow gate
is wet there will be
rain.

Stonemasons
put stones on display
barbers sweep clippings into a pile
commentators lost the
thread.

Meanwhile
the wind has turned
along the street a blackbird
sings.

BP

SILJA WALTER

DIE TÄNZERIN

Der Tanz ist aus. Mein Herz ist süss wie Nüsse,
Und was ich denke, blüht mir aus der Haut.
Wenn ich jetzt sacht mir in die Knöchel bisse,
Sie röchen süsser als der Sud Melisse,
Der rot und klingend in der Kachel braut.

Sprich nicht von Tanz und nicht von Mond und Baum
Und ja nicht von der Seele, sprich jetzt nicht.
Mein Kleid hat einen riesenbreiten Saum,
Damit bedeck ich Füsse und Gesicht
Und alles, was in diesem Abend kauert,
Aus jedem Flur herankriecht und mich misst
Mit grauem Blick, sich duckt und mich belauert,
Mich gellend anfällt und mein Antlitz küsst.

Sprich nicht von Tanz und nicht von Stern und Traum
Und ja nicht von der Seele, lass uns schweigen.
Mein Kleid hat einen riesenbreiten Saum,
Drin ruht verwahrt der Dinge Sinn und Reigen.

Ich wollte Schnee sein, mitten im August,
Und langsam von den Rändern her vergehn,
Langsam mich selbst vergessend, ich hätt Lust,
Dabei mir selber singend zuzusehn.

SILJA WALTER

THE DANCER

The dance is over. My heart is sweet as a nut,
And all that I think blooms from my skin.
If I were to bite my knuckle now gingerly,
The smell would be sweeter than lemon balm,
brewing red and tinkling on the tile stove.

Don't speak of the dance, nor of moon or tree,
And certainly not of the soul, don't speak now.
My dress has a very wide hem,
It covers my face and my feet
And everything that cowers this night,
That creeps out from corridors and sizes me up
With a dreadful look, that cringes and stalks,
That accosts me shrilly and kisses my cheek.

Don't speak of the dance, nor of stars or dreams,
And certainly not of the soul, let's not speak at all.
My dress has a very wide hem,
Under which I keep safe the meaning and the ways of things.

I wanted to be snow in the middle of August,
And to melt slowly from the periphery inward,
Slowly forgetting myself, I'd have wanted
At the same time to have watched myself, singing.

RM

KURT MARTI

"DEM HERRN UNSEREM GOTT . . ."

dem herrn unserem gott
hat es ganz und gar nicht gefallen
dass gustav e. lips
durch einen verkehrsunfall starb

erstens war er zu jung
zweitens seiner frau ein zärtlicher mann
drittens zwei kindern ein lustiger vater
viertens den freunden ein guter freund
fünftens erfüllt von vielen ideen

was soll jetzt ohne ihn werden?
was ist seine frau ohne ihn?
wer spielt mit den kindern?
wer ersetzt einen freund?
wer hat die neuen ideen?

dem herrn unserem gott
hat es ganz und gar nicht gefallen
dass einige von euch dachten
es habe ihm solches gefallen

im namen dessen der tote erweckte
im namen des toten der auferstand:
wir protestieren gegen den tod von gustav e. lips

KURT MARTI

"IT DID NOT PLEASE THE LORD . . ."

it did not please the lord
our god at all
that gustav e. lips
died in an automobile accident

first he was too young
second too tender a husband to his wife
third too joyful a father of two children
fourth to his friends too good a friend
fifth too full of ideas

what will happen now without him?
what will happen to his wife?
who will play with his children?
what replaces a friend?
who has any ideas?

it did not please the lord
our god at all
that some of you thought
such a thing might have pleased him

in the name of him who raised the dead
in the name of the dead who arose:
we protest the death of gustav e. lips

HOMMAGE À RABELAIS

d'schöni
vo de wüeschte wörter
isch e brunne
i dr wüeschti
vo de schöne wörter

WIE GEITS?

äs chunnt
äs geit

ganz zerscht
chunnt meh
als geit

doch gly
chunnts so
wies geit

und bald
geit meh
als chunnt

bis
alles geit
und nüt me chunnt

HOMMAGE À RABELAIS

the loveliest
of the ugliest words
is like a fountain
in a desert
of the loveliest words

HOW'S IT GOING?

it comes
it goes

mostly
more comes
than goes

although
it comes
as it goes

soon enough
more goes
than comes

until
it's all gone
and nothing more comes

WO CHIEMTE MER HI?

wo chiemte mer hi
wenn alli seite
wo chiemte mer hi
und niemer giengti
für einisch z'luege
wohi dass me chiem
we me gieng

Z. B. 25.11.72

hütt
am morge
d'mäldig
geschter
am aabe
sygi
dr mani

dr mani matter
sygi
tödlech

usgrächnet är

WHERE WOULD WE BE?

where would we be
if everyone said
where would we be
and no one went
to see
where we'd be
if we'd gone

E.G., 11/25/72

today
in the morning
the message
yesterday
in the night
mani apparently
was

mani matter
was
mortal

he of all people

RM

ERIKA BURKART

DIE TOTEN

Erst sind sie ganz klein,
stehen wie Puppen
auf deiner Schwelle.

Sie wachsen
von Neumond zu Neumond,
in immer anderen Masken
dringen sie ein in den Traum
und fordern von dir
ihren Löwenanteil.

Sie wärmen die Hände
am offenen Feuer
draussen im Westen
unter dem sinkenden Sternbild.

In Flechten und Flecken
erkennst du sie wieder,
unterm Schattenhut
und im Schleier von Schnee,
ihre Aschenspur gehst du,
gehst ihre Windspur,
die Finsternis summt
von ihren Stimmen in dir.

ERIKA BURKART

THE DEAD

They're very small at first,
standing like dolls
on your doorstep.

They grow,
from new moon to new moon,
always in other masks,
intrude on your dream
and demand of you
the lion's share.

They warm their hands
at open fires
out west
where constellations sink.

In lichen and in dappled light
you recognize them,
brimmed in shadow,
enshrouded in snow,
you trace their ash path,
follow their scent,
the darkness drones,
from their voices, in you.

RM

ALEXANDER XAVER GWERDER

DAMALS

Die Blätter fielen stiller
als je in solcher Nacht.
Die Heimkehr nach dem Thriller,
die Blätter fielen stiller,
hat mich so müd gemacht.

Es roch nach Laub und Larven.
Entsinnst du dich—, damals,
als wir uns nachts bewarfen,
es roch nach Lehm und Larven,
auch kroch's dir in den Hals?

Entlang der langen Mauer
beim Neubau, hinter Brettern
ein Kuss, ein Gassenhauer—,
dazu die nasse Mauer
und jetzt so still Entblättern . . .

Nun wirst du wo sein? Sieh,
es ist dieselbe Nacht!
Doch dass ich später nie—
Nun wirst du wo sein? Sieh:
Ich hab an dich gedacht.
Damals wird uns noch bleiben.
Damals ist ein Geruch
nach heimatlosem Treiben—
Erinnern, Träume, Schreiben,
gepresstes Blatt im Buch.

ALEXANDER XAVER GWERDER

BACK THEN

The leaves fell softer
than ever that night.
The walk home after the thriller,
the leaves falling softer,
made me tired.

It smelled like leaves and larvae.
Do you remember—back then,
nights we'd throw ourselves at each other,
it smelled like loam and larvae,
did it catch in your throat, too?

Along the long wall
past construction, behind boards,
a kiss, a pop song playing—
and the damp wall
and softly, ourselves defoliating . . .

Where are you now? Look,
this is that night, too!
It's true I never did—
Where are you now? Look,
I've thought of you.
Back then will remain with us.
Back then is a fragrance
of vagrant urges—
dreams, writing, remembrance,
a leaf pressed between pages.

ICH GEH UNTER LAUTER SCHATTEN

Was ist denn das für eine Zeit—
Die Wälder sind voll von Traumgetier.
Wenn ich nur wüsste, wer immer so schreit.
Weiss nicht einmal, ob es regnet oder schneit,
ob du erfrierst auf dem Weg zu mir—

Die Wälder sind voll von Traumgetier,
ich geh unter lauter Schatten—
Es sind Netze gespannt von dir zu mir,
und was sich drin fängt, ist nicht von hier,
ist, was wir längst vergessen hatten.

Wenn ich nur wüsste, wer immer so schreit?
Ich sucht ihm ein wenig zu geben
von jenem stillen Trunk zu zweit,
voll Taumel und voll Seligkeit
würd ich den Becher ihm heben—

Weiss nicht einmal, ob es schneit oder regnet . . .
Sah die Sterne nicht mehr, seit ich dich verliess;
kenn den Weg nicht mehr, den du mir gesegnet,
und zweifle sogar, ob du mir begegnet—
Wer war denn das, der mich gehen hiess?

Aber, du findest doch her zu mir—?
Sieh, es wird Zeit, dass ich ende.
Die Wälder sind voll von Traumgetier
und ich darunter, bin nicht von hier . . .
Ich gäb alles, wenn ich dich fände!

I'M WALKING AMONG ALL THESE SHADOWS

What hour is this—
The woods are alive with dream beasts,
If only I knew who's there, screaming.
I don't even know, though, if it's raining or snowing,
or if, on your way to me, you're freezing—

The woods are alive with dream beasts,
and I'm walking among all these shadows—
There are nets that stretch out between us,
and what they ensnare is not of this place,
it's what we've forgotten long ago.

If only I knew who's there, screaming.
I sought him to give him
a quenching drink, the two of us,
a draft full of rapture, of bliss,
I would hold the glass to his lips—

I don't even know, though, if it's raining or snowing . . .
I've seen no more stars since I left you,
lost the way, the one you blessed for me,
and begin to doubt you will happen upon me—
Who was it who told me to go?

But you will make your way back to me—?
Look, it's time now I put an end to
this, the woods alive with dream beasts
and I among them, I'm not of this place . . .
I'd give everything to find you.

RM

EUGEN GOMRINGER

VIELLEICHT

vielleicht baum
baum vielleicht

vielleicht vogel
vogel vielleicht

vielleicht frühling
frühling vielleicht

vielleicht worte
worte vielleicht

"SCHWEIGEN SCHWEIGEN SCHWEIGEN . . ."

schweigen schweigen schweigen
schweigen schweigen schweigen
schweigen   schweigen
schweigen schweigen schweigen
schweigen schweigen schweigen

EUGEN GOMRINGER

PERHAPS

perhaps tree
tree perhaps

perhaps bird
bird perhaps

perhaps spring
spring perhaps

perhaps words
words perhaps

"BE STILL BE STILL BE STILL . . ."

be still   be still   be still
be still   be still   be still
be still   be still
be still   be still   be still
be still   be still   be still

SCHWIIZER

luege
aaluege
zueluege

nöd rede
sicher sii
nu luege
nüd znäch
nu vu wiitem
ruig bliibe

schwiizer sii
schwiizer bliibe
nu luege

SWISS

look
watch
spectate

don't speak
keep safe
just look
don't get too close
keep back
hush

to be swiss
to keep swiss
just look

RM

ADELHEID DUVANEL

WIND

Wiegt Wolkenweiber, gräbt Wasser um
Neidet den trunkenen Fischen den Traum
Weckt alle Feuer, rupft leer den Baum
Raubt aus dem Hause der Kranken den Schrei
Verachtet Gräber, jagt fort den Mond
Verstopft dem Vogel den Schnabel mit Schnee
Umschleicht den Turm, kitzelt die Glocke
Flösst kalte, weisse Blumen zu Tal.

FLUCHT

Reiss die Etikette weg
es ist Zeit, zu fliehen
die Marktplätze sind leer
Falt die Flügel überm Kopf
die Himmelsschale bricht
Sterne schlüpfen aus
stürzen ab, schade
sie singt nicht
Deine Astgabelstimme.

ADELHEID DUVANEL

WIND

Makes wisps of cloud-women, ripples water
Envies the drunken fish their dream
Wakes fire, whips the tree bare
Steals the wails of the ailing from their home
Defiles graves, hounds away the moon
Crams the bird's beak full of snow
Prowls around towers, tickles the bells
Floats cold white petals to the valley floor.

ESCAPE

Tear the labels off
Now is the time to flee
The markets are empty
Fold your wings overhead
Heaven's cup ruptures
Stars slip from it,
Plummet, pity
It don't sing,
Your tree-crook voice.

RM

ELISABETH MEYLAN

BLAISE CENDRARS

Er entwich aus dem Fenster,
um ein Leben lang
die Schule zu schwänzen.

Eine Erstausgabe von Villon
in der Tasche
durchreiste er die Welt.

Er erkannte die Länder
blindlings,
an ihrem Geruch.

Den Kreml sah er als
riesigen,
mit Gold überbackenen
Tartarenkuchen.

Seinen Rennwagen fuhr er mit der Linken.
(Die Rechte hatte er im Krieg verloren)

Er hatte Lavater, Euler
und Thomas Platter
zu seinen Vorfahren ernannt.

Mit sechzig
erschien ihm die Verwandtschaft
jedoch ungewiss.

ELISABETH MEYLAN

BLAISE CENDRARS

He escaped out the window
in order to cut
class his whole life long.

He traveled the world,
in his pocket
a first edition of Villon.

He perceived countries
blindly
by their scent.

The Kremlin he saw as
colossal
Tartar cakes
scalloped in gold.

With his left hand he steered the racecar.
(His right he'd lost in the war.)

He had Lavater, Euler
and Thomas Platter
appointed his ancestors.

Though at sixty
the kinship seemed to him
uncertain.

RM

NIKLAUS MEIENBERG

ELEGIE ÜBER DEN ZUFALL DER GEBURT

Für Blaise Cendrars

Das zufällige Land
Wo ich der Mutter entfiel
Ausgestossen abgeschnitten eingewickelt
im Mutterland
der befleckten Empfängnis
O mein Heimatland
O mein Vaterland
Mit dem Muttermal
Der motherfucker
Weshalb z. B. nicht in Corpus Christi
Auch Thule wäre
ein möglicher Ort
Ultima Thule
Weshalb liess sie mich
in diese Falle fallen
Zwischen Zwetschgenköpfe
Ins unerhörte Zwitscherland
Gelandet durch Zufall
in diesem Nichtland
Wo die Spitzbäuche die Rundköpfe bespitzeln
abgesondert
auf diesen fleissigen Fleck
diesen sauren Landstrich
Hominid
Unter Hominiden

NIKLAUS MEIENBERG

ELEGY ON THE ACCIDENT OF BIRTH

for Blaise Cendrars

The accidental country
Into which my mother expelled me
Cast out cut off and swaddled
In the Motherland
Of a maculate conception
O my Homeland
O my Fatherland
Mother-marked from birth
The *motherfucker*
Why not Corpus Christi for instance
Even Thule might have been
A probable place
Ultima Thule, the ends of the earth
Why could she not have borne me
Somewhere more bearable than this
Abandoned here among birdbrains
In this fantastic yellow-bellied Twitcherland
Landed by accident
In this insipid Swindlerland
Where the Paunchbellies spy on the Roundheads
Sequestered
In this punctilious spot
This upright, uptight place
A hominid
Among hominids

Weshalb nicht ausgebrütet
in Feuerland Apulien Sierra Leone
Weshalb in diesem Rentnernationalpark
Im Binnenland das an seiner Vergangenheit lutscht
Weshalb nicht empfing sie mich im Kreuz des Südens
statt unter diesem unempfänglichen bleichen Kreuz
zu dem sie täglich kriechen
warum nicht trug sie mich nach Massachusetts
bevor ich ausgetragen war
Oder British Columbia wo die Ebene glänzt
Oder staatenlose Meergeburt
auf der MS Tübingen
abgenabelt vor Neufundland
schaumgeboren salzgesegnet

oder brüllend erschienen
in einer Transatlantikconcorde
aber nicht der SWISSAIR

Weshalb hat sie mich
in diesem Loch geworfen
Wo Berge sich erheben
Wie Bretter vor dem Kopf

Why not have been hatched
In Tierra del Fuego, Apulia, Sierra Leone
Why here in this pensioner's national park
Landlocked and sucking its past like a thumb
Why could she not have conceived me under the Southern Cross
Instead of in the shadow of this one, sallow, insensate
Under which they grovel each day
Why not have carried me to Massachusetts
Before delivering me up
Or British Columbia, or some fruited plain
Or a stateless birth at sea
On the MS *Tübingen*
My cord cut before Newfoundland
Borne on the foam, salt-washed

Or come screaming into the world
Aboard a transatlantic Concorde
Though not SWISSAIR

Why did she have to whelp me
Into this hole
Where the mountains rise up
Like boards in front of your face

RM

FELIX PHILIPP INGOLD

HIMMELSKUNDE

Nicht wahr ist
das Haar der Berenike. Nike
wartet auf den Sieg
der sie einst selber war.
Vergebens. Ens
ist sächlich also auch nicht
wahrer. Klar erkennt man
das Design des
Bösen war schon immer
unsichtbar. Armada aber schön
in nächster Ferne. Sterne
nämlich die so stur die Ewigkeit
behaupten sind nichts anderes
als was. Fossiles
Licht.

FELIX PHILIPP INGOLD

ASTRONOMY

It's not real,
Berenike's hair. Nike still
waiting for the victory
that once she was herself.
In vain. *Ens*
is neuter therefore not
any more real. Clearly
one sees evil's design
has always been
invisible. Armada are pretty
in the near distance. Stars too
stubbornly implying eternity
yet are nothing other
than something. Fossilized
light.

WETTERKARTE

Unser Hoch verlagert sich
nach Ostern.
Die Ewigkeit (man sieht sie links
im Bild als schwarzes Loch) nimmt langsam
ab und wird Geschichte.
Die Nullgradgrenze liegt auf halber
Höhe zwischen Knie
und Kinn. Das heisst sie hält
so ungefähr die Mitte.
Was. Dein Land hat jetzt genau
die Grösse und
die Nacktheit meiner Hand.
Und. Übermorgen
ist bereits gewesen. Gestern auch. Doch
gestern gab's die Zukunft noch. Das
Nichts. Und heute nichts
als diese süsse Kälte.
                              Aus unsern
Namen emigrieren die Vokale
in die menschenleere
Umgangssprache.

WEATHER MAP

Our high shifts, slouches
toward Easter.
Eternity (here on the left
of the screen, a black hole)
diminishes slowly
and becomes history.
The freezing point is lying at mid-
elevation between knee
and chin. That means it's holding
at about center.
That. Your country is now exactly
the size and nakedness of my hand.
And. The day after tomorrow
has already been. Yesterday too.
Though yesterday there was still the future.
The void. And today nothing
but this sweet cold.
                              From our
names the vowels are emigrating,
into the uninhabited
vernacular.

RM

BERNADETTE LERJEN-SARBACH

VILICHT

redt üs mier
mini Müetter
mini Grossmüetter
oder äs ganzus Volch

MÜET ZUM EIGENU

Jetz hesch lang gnüeg
Lieder va anneru gsungu
Los in dich
und de sing äntli
dini Melodii

BIM SCHRIIBU

Wenn
ich
eleinzig bi
sid
ier
alli
da

BERNADETTE LERJEN-SARBACH

MAYBE

speaks from me
my mother
my grandmother
or the entire nation

COURAGE FOR ONESELF

Now you long enough have sung
the songs of everyone other
Listen within
and finally sing
a melody of your own

WHEN I WRITE

Whenever
I'm
all alone
you
are
all
here

RM

KLAUS MERZ

ZURÜSTERIN NACHT

Manchmal vor Tag
wird mir das Leben
zugänglich bis tief
in die Kindheit hinab.

Narben glimmen auf
ein Vers kühlt sie ab
mit Regen, mit Schnee.

Zukunft bleibt flüchtig
nur die Toten sind nah.
Und die Gegenwart
verliert ihr Gewicht.

GROSSE NACHT

Alles ist da: das Meer
die Skyline, dein Herz-
schlag am Ohr. Und
in Karakorum, hört man
setze Dschingis Khan
seine Reiterheere wieder
in Trab: Bringt mir Bilder
vom Mars, befiehlt er
den Scharen, zieh los
Ögedei!

KLAUS MERZ

PREPARER, NIGHT

Sometimes before daybreak
my life seems to me
accessible as far back
as childhood.

Scars flare up,
verse cools them off
with rain, with snow.

The future remains fugitive
only the dead are near.
And presence
loses its substance.

MAGNIFICENT NIGHT

Everything's here: the sea
the skyline, your heart-
beat in my ear.
And in Karakorum, they say
Genghis Khan
is sending his riders
out again: bring me pictures
from Mars, he orders
the troops: off with you,
Ögedei!

RM

URS ALLEMANN

SELBSTPORTRÄT IM GEÄST

Ich
im Baumschiff
Sterbeäpfel zählend

Geborner Herbsttyp
Nebelohr für Selbsteinschläferungsweisen
Fallobstmanie

Im Windchanson
abge-
stotterte Totenkopfernte

O aber
unfrei um mich assoziiert
Hirntropfenglitzern

Schädeltau
Innen-Aussen-Schnappschüsse
mit Umstülptrick

Und unten Erd-
Bartstoppeln dass
treffsicher drauf zu geweint wird

URS ALLEMANN

SELF-PORTRAIT IN THE BRANCHES

I
in the tree-ship
reckoning death-apples

Inborn autumnist
fog-ear for self-soporific technique
obsession with stoop fruit

Harvest of death's-heads paid
down in wind-
chanson installments

But oh
all around me, unfree, mingle
glimmers of brain-dripping

Skull-dew
internal-and-external snapshots
prepared for inversion

And down below, five-
o'clock soil-shadow, wept
upon accurately

AARON KERNER

ARMIN SENSER

GROSSES ERWACHEN

Ich erwache. Alles ringsum erwacht.
Decke, Wand, Türe, Vorhänge, Tische,
der Boden, Stühle erwachen. Wimpern,
Haare, Arme, der Nacken, Rücken,
Bauch, Hüfte, Schenkel, Waden, Gelenke,
Knöchel, Zehen, Nägel, Finger erwachen.
Es erwachen Lippen, Zunge, Gaumen,
das Gähnen, der Bauchnabel, Nasenflügel,
das Bewusstsein erwacht, der Raum, die
Zeit erwachen, alles erwacht. Dinge und
Menschen. Liegen, Sitzen, Stehen, Torkeln,
Halten erwachen. Das Blut erwacht und
der Atem. Der Lichtschalter, Spiegel,
die Blendung, das Zwinkern, Zähne,
Zahnfleisch, Falten, Bart, Unterhose—Penis
und Urin erwachen. Es erwacht ein Fluch,
ein Wort, ein Blick erwachen. Farben.
Beine übereinandergeschlagen, der Brustansatz.
Ein Stück Nacht erwacht und ein Fetzen Traum.

Prag ist erwacht und Rom. Der ganze Balkan
erwacht. Und Afrika erwacht von Süd nach
Nord. Schanghai erwacht nach Peking, aus dem
Schlaf gerüttelt von zitternder Hand. Leningrad
erwachte in einem Zug, auch Stalingrad. Linz
ist erwacht, dann München, Berlin—die ganze
Welt. Niemand schläft. Kein Mensch. Dinge
schlafen nicht. Auch nicht Tiere.
Erwacht ist alles. Nichts das schläft.

ARMIN SENSER

GREAT AWAKENING

I wake up and all around me everything is waking.
Walls, doors, curtains, tables, and chairs,
the ceiling and floor are waking up. Eyelashes.
Hair, arms, neck, back,
belly, hips, thighs, calves,
joints, knuckles, toes, nails, fingers are waking up.
Lips are waking, tongue, palate,
the fact of yawning, the bellybutton,
nostrils and consciousness wake up, the room,
time, everything is waking. Things and
people. Lying wakes up, and sitting, standing, staggering,
stopping are waking. The blood wakes and
breath. The light switch, the mirror,
the glare and twinkle, teeth,
gums, wrinkles, beard, underwear—penis
and urine wake up. A curse is awakened,
awakened are a word, a look. Colors.
Legs crossed, cleavage.
A piece of night wakes and a scrap of dream.

Prague is awake and Rome. The whole of the Balkans
is awake. And Africa wakes from south to
north. Shanghai wakes after Peking, shaken from
sleep by a trembling hand. Leningrad
awoke all at once, Stalingrad too. Linz
is awake, then Munich, Berlin—the entire
world. No one is sleeping. No man. Things
are not sleeping. Nor are the animals.
Everything is awake. There's nothing that sleeps.

Montag, Dienstag, Mittwoch, Donnerstag,
Freitag und Samstag erwachen. Auch
heute und morgen, Hemd und Hosen,
Kaffee, Tee, das Geschirr erwachen.
Gequietsche, Geklirre, Blubbern, Schlurfen
erwachen und Adjektive, Verben im
Indikativ und Konditional. Es erwacht der
Ablativ, Vokativ und jedes Motiv.
Alles ist da—ist wach. Nichts kennt mehr
den Schlaf. Auch er ist erwacht mit dem
Unbewussten und mit den Geheimnissen.
Der Nebel erwacht und die Dämmerung,
der Sonnenschein, Wolken, der Sturm, der
Hurrikan. Treppen erwachen, Strassen
erwachen, Plätze mit Statuen, Kugeln,
Toten und Kanonen, Panzern, Liebespaaren.
Häuser sind erwacht und Kamine, von
Ost nach West mit einem bitteren Geruch.
Antennen erwachen, Nachrichten, Schatten,
Wärme und Kälte. Wasser, Eis, Gase
im Äther und in Lungen. Atome erwachen
und die Radioaktivität. Wahrscheinlichkeit
und Statistiken erwachen zugleich mit allen
Zahlen, Gesetzen, Regeln und Fehlern.

Niemand kann seine Augen schliessen.
Alles wird wach. Ob Materie oder Seele,
Engel oder Potentat. Und Wissen erwacht.
Auch das Vergessen und mit ihm
erwacht Erinnerung, Verbrechen,
Grausamkeiten und Freiheit, Neid
und Einsamkeit. Der Rassismus, der
noch schläft erwacht. Sekten, Pamphlete,

Monday, Tuesday, Wednesday, Thursday
Friday, and Saturday wake up. And
today and tomorrow, shirt and pants,
coffee, tea, the dishes wake up.
Squeaking, clanking, mumbling, slurping,
these are waking, and adjectives, verbs in the
indicative and the conditional. Waking up:
the ablative, vocative, and every motive.
Everything is here—is awake. Nothing knows
sleep anymore. Even sleep itself is awake, along with
the unconscious and the arcane.
Fog wakes up and twilight,
sunshine, clouds, the storm, the hurricane.
Stairs wake up, streets wake up,
parks with statues, bullets, canons,
and the dead wake too, and tanks, and lovers.
Houses are awake and chimneys,
from east to west with an acrid smell.
Antennae wake up, news, shadows,
warm and cold. Water, ice, gas
in ether and in the lungs. Atoms wake up
and radioactivity. Probability
and statistics are waking up in unison with
all numbers, laws, rules, and errors.

No one can keep his eyes closed.
Everything is waking. Whether substance or spirit,
angel or potentate. And knowledge wakes up.
And forgetting too, and with it
awakes memory, crime,
atrocities and freedom, envy
and loneliness. Racism that
had gone on sleeping now wakes. Cults, pamphlets,

Lethe erwachen, Styx und Dante.
Väter erwachen, Mütter, Kinder, Föten,
Spermen, Eizellen, alle Verwandten.
Freunde erwachen, Kränkungen, das
Lachen. Wünsche erwachen, erfüllte
und unerfüllte und wecken Schicksale.
Geweckt werden Katastrophen, Ehen
und ihre Kombinationen. Es erwachen
die Möglichkeiten und Wirklichkeiten.
Es stehen auf Zukunft, Vergangenheit
und Gegenwart, einander gleichgestellt.

Aufgewacht sind auch Laute, Babel
und Sprachen. Gesang und Lieder.
Madrigale. Sonette. Die Oper. Verse.
Alles erwacht unverhofft gerade
jetzt. Strophen erwachen, der Versuch,
der Roman erwachen und Entwürfe.
Allesamt aufgewacht in Bibliotheken,
im Hörer, Leser, Verleger, im Autor—
in Gedanken, auf dem Papier, in Tinte,
Stein, auf kleiner runder Scheibe sind
erwacht die Grosse Elegie für John Donne,
Gezählte Tage, der Brief an Lord Byron,
der Divan, Spaziergang, die Bukolik,
Epoden und alle Vaginen und Hoden.
Noah erwacht und die Ertrunkenen,
Abraham, Paulus und Saulus erwachen,
David und das Kind. Maria, schwanger
auf der Flucht. Und die fliehenden Völker.
Sie tauchen auf—erwacht wie alle Sklaven
und Sokrates, Platon, Descartes, Spinoza
und Kant, Epikur erwacht auch. Alle Philosophen,
die Ideen erwachen. Ans Licht tritt alles.

and the Lethe wakes up, the River Styx, and Dante.
Fathers wake up and mothers, children, fetuses,
sperm, ova, everything kindred.
Friends wake up, illnesses,
laughter. Wishes wake up, fulfilled
and unfulfilled, and rouse the fates.
Catastrophes are awakened, marriages
in their various combinations. Possibilities
and realities are being awoken.
Future, past, and present are standing
on equal terms with one another.

Sound too has awoken, Babel
and languages. Chanting and song.
Madrigals. Sonnets. The opera. Verse.
Everything is waking, unforeseen, right
now. Stanzas wake up, the attempt,
the novel wakes, and drafts and drafts.
All of it, awaking in libraries,
in the listener, reader, publisher, in the author—
awaking in thought, on paper, in ink,
stone, on small thin leaves the great
elegies for John Donne have woken up,
numbered days, the letter to Lord Byron,
the Divan, long walks, the pastoral,
epodes, and every vagina, every testicle.
Noah wakes up as well as the drowned,
Abraham, Paul, and Saul wake up,
David and the child. Mary, pregnant
and on the run. And all the fleeing peoples.
They arise—awakened like each and every slave
and Socrates, Plato, Descartes, Spinoza
and Kant, even Epicurus is awake. All the philosophers
that wake the ideas. Everything is coming to light.

Erwacht nach dem langen Schlaf, erwacht
nach kurzem Leben und langem Alter,
erwacht nackt, in Hütten, Stiefeln, im
Feld, Blut, Morast. Erwacht beim Liebesakt.
Erwacht, erwacht, erwacht. Und erwacht.

Aale, Wale, Archäopteryxe sind erwacht,
Schnecken, Schlangen und deren Entwurf.
Dinosaurier erwachen. Die Eis-, Würm-,
Permzeit erwachen—gute und schlechte
Zeiten, die Grossen Erwartungen erwachen.
Geweckt werden Napoleoniden und jede Krone.
Miles erwacht und Bach, Mozart und Dvořák.
Jede Schlacht. Vietnam erwacht, Korea,
der Golf, die beiden und alle anderen Kriege.

Du bist erwacht und ich. Und erwacht sind
Planeten, Sterne, Sonnen, Monde, Galaxien
und Universen. Die Alpen, Karpaten, der
Himalaja sind erwacht. Tibet ist erwacht, das
Baskenland, Istrien, Galizien und der Schwarzwald.
Erwacht sind Knossos, Pompeji, die
Azteken, Inuit und Korsen. Buddhisten,
Hindus, Sikhs, Schiiten, Sunniten
sind auch erwacht und Christen, Juden und
Schwule, Technokraten, Börsianer,
Zuhälter und Richter, Polizisten und
Lehrer. Alle erwacht, alle ausnahmslos.

Aufgeschreckt sind Schrauben, Bleche,
Reifen, Ziegel, Backsteine, der Beton,
Stahl und Holz. Züge, Flugzeuge,
Auto- und Solarmobile, Fahrräder,

Awoken after the long sleep, after
a short life and a long old age,
awoke naked, in huts, in boots, in
fields, blood, the mire. Awakened while making love.
Awake, awake, awake. And awake.

Eels, whales, archaeopteryxes have all woken up,
snails, snakes, and their rough drafts.
The dinosaurs are waking now. The Ice, Bronze,
and Stone Ages awake—good eras and bad,
great expectations are waking.
The Bonapartes are roused and every crown.
Miles wakes up and Bach, Mozart, and Dvořák.
Every battle. Vietnam wakes up, Korea,
the Persian Gulf, both of them, and every other war.

You are awake and so am I. And awake now too
are planets, stars, suns, moons, galaxies,
and universes. The Alps, Carpathians, the
Himalayas are awake. Tibet is awake, the
Basque country, Istria, Galicia, and the Black Forest.
Awake now are Knossos, Pompeii, the
Aztecs, Inuit, and Corsicans. Buddhists,
Hindus, Sikhs, Shi'ites, Sunnis
are all awake, and Christians and Jews,
queers, technocrats, venture capitalists,
pimps and judges, teachers and police.
All are awake, all without exception.

Startled awake now are screws, sheet metal,
tires, tiles, bricks and mortar,
steel and wood. Trains, airplanes,
diesel and solar cars, bicycles,

Traktoren, Lastwagen, sie alle sind
erwacht. Und Schiffe. Mit ihnen
erwachen Abgase, Unfälle, Steuern,
Einkommen, Reisen, Spesen, Tankstellen,
Flughäfen, Landestege und Havarien,
Öltanker und Flugzeugträger.

Die Welt ist erwacht. Mittag, Nachmittag,
der Morgen, die Dämmerung, die Nacht.
Es erwacht das Einschlafen, Schlummern,
Schnarchen. Der Mond erwacht, Sternschnuppen,
Satelliten, Astronauten und Asteroiden
erwachen. Die Stille erwacht. Erwacht ist
der Lärm. Von Elementarteilchen bis
zu den Augen ist alles offen. Verschlossen
ist nichts, nichts verborgen, nichts
verloren. Alles ist gefunden, erwacht.

Und Gott ist erwacht. Jedes Prinzip. Und Theorien.
Nichts ist tot. Weder Stein, Baum noch
Einfall, Empfindung oder Verdauung
schlafen. Auch Namenloses schläft nicht.

Alles ist da, erwacht, du und ich. Er, sie und
es. Um uns herum, um Dinge und Menschen,
steht das Erwachen, greifbar, sicht- und fühlbar
nah. Vom grossen Erwachen erfasst auch
das Warten, dass der Augenblick ewig schien.
Ewig erwacht, alles, denn es ist der Jüngste Tag.

tractors and semi trucks, all of these are
awake. And ships. And these awake
along with them exhaust, accidents, taxes,
income, travel, expenses, gas stations,
airports, harbors, and damages,
oil tankers and aircraft carriers.

The world is awake. Midday, afternoon,
morning, twilight, the night.
Awake now are falling asleep, napping,
snoring. The moon wakes up, meteors,
satellites, astronauts and asteroids
are waking up now. Silence wakes. Awake now
is noise. From elementary particles right up to
your eyes, everything is open. Nothing
is closed, nothing is hidden, nothing
lost. All is found, awake.

And God is awake. Every principle. And theories.
Nothing is dead. Neither stone nor tree, nor
passing notion, neither sensation nor digestion are
asleep any longer. Even the nameless doesn't sleep.

Everything is present, awake. You and I. He, she, and
it. All around us, around things and people—
there is the awakening, graspably, visibly, sensibly
near. Gathered up in the great awakening is
the waiting, too, so that the moment seems an eternity.
Eternity is awake, all of it, as the hour has now grown late.

                                                              RM

ROLF HERMANN

HOMMAGE AN DAS RÜCKENSCHWIMMEN
IN DER NÄHE VON CHICAGO UND ANDERSWO

Das Leben beginnt in einer 0.75l
Thermosflasche die ich auf dem
Bauch trage den Flüssen entgegen
schwimme und dich oh Fernseh
Grossmutter verehre four double
shots of espresso please jedes
Gemälde gräbt etwas in mir aus
ich bleibe stehen in einem grossen
viel verzweigten Saal die bis zum
Rand gefüllten Schubladen weit aus
meinem Brustkorb hängend küsse
all jenen die Hände die eine Grossstadt
in eine Schuhschachtel packen die
schmutzigen Fassaden des Hafenviertels
die Falter im Licht surrender Neonröhren
wenn ich in einer leeren Lagerhalle
Seekarten zerreisse also nichts wie
weiter und links um die Ecke auf die
eingerahmten Gletscher zu deren
Zungen am Äquator liegen wo ich die
Augen schliesse um sie zu öffnen

ROLF HERMANN

AN HOMAGE TO BACKSTROKE SWIMMING
NEAR CHICAGO AND ELSEWHERE

Life begins in a 25-ounce
thermos flask that I carry on
my belly against the rivers
I swim and you oh television
grandmother I adore vier espressi
doppi cun lat s'il vous plaît every
painting digs out something in me
I remain standing in a large
much-too-extended hall the
drawers filled to the brim hanging
far out of my chest I kiss the hands
of all those that pack a city
into a shoebox the filthy façades
of the harbor district the moths
in the humming light of neon strips
when I rip up sea charts in an empty
warehouse there's nothing like
onwards and left around the corner
to the framed glaciers whose
tongues lie on the equator where
I close my eyes to open them

TRANSLATED BY ELIZABETH VICK-HERMANN AND THE AUTHOR

RAPHAEL URWEIDER

MANUFAKTUREN (*Auszüge*)

in der milde des nachmittags liegen
die kontinente beieinander wie schläfrige

kühe die wiesen der ozeane sind sehr blau
mister magellan zeichnet in sein geheimes

tagebuch die kontinente räkeln sich
in der milde des abends mister magellans

seekarten sind schattenrisse von heimischem
vieh wie auch träume der spanischen

königin in der milde der nacht nähren sich
die kontinente an den wiesen der ebbe

an den wiesen der flut mister magellan
skizziert die küstenlinien der kühe

in der milde des morgens schimmern
die noch leeren seiten des magellanschen

tagebuches weit heller als die träume der
königin wie frischmilch der kontinente

                *

herr galilei ist der grosse erfinder von
sonne mond und sternen einer vogelvoliere

RAPHAEL URWEIDER

from MANUFACTURES

placid in the afternoon the continents
are lying side by side like drowsing

cows the ocean meadows are very blue
mister magellan is sketching in his secret

diary meanwhile the continents are sprawling
into the placid evening mister magellan's

maps are silhouettes of native beasts
and dreams of the spanish queen

in the placid night the continents
feed on meadows of low tide

on meadows of high tide mister magellan
outlines the coastlines of cows

placid in the morning the still
empty pages of magellan's diary

shimmer far brighter than dreams of the queen
like the fresh milk of the continents

*

mister galileo is the great discoverer
of sun moon stars of an aviary

entspringen die gelernten gedanken der
papageie herr galilei blickt durch sein

erdichtetes fernrohr er beobachtet nachtvögel
schläft tagsüber ihm kommen sternfarbene

papageie in die träume herr galilei putzt
die linsen des teleskops mit hirschleder

auch abends wiederholen sich die parolen
der papageie er hört sie nicht und richtet

seine gedanken nach den sternen was braucht
er da papageie herr galilei reinigt seinen

blick mir hirschleder erfindet sonne mond
und deren gefolgschaft träumt wie in

gedanken von nachtvögeln er wünscht
sich tagsüber ein sternfarbenes federkleid

*

guten tag herr gutenberg spricht ein mainzer
winzer er zwinkert dem meister zweiäugig zu

er weiss der gutenberg druckt weisheiten
aus weinpressen das schwarz und weiss ist

meister johanns sache während sie hinab
in den keller steigen tauschen sie druckreife

news aus der winzer lässt das winzern er ist
zwinkernder geselle gutenbergs geworden

his learned thoughts arise like parrots
mister galileo is looking through

his fabled telescope watching the night birds
sleeping by day star-colored parrots

come to him in dreams mister galileo cleans
the lens of his telescope with chamois

nights too the parrots repeat their calls
he does not hear them and turns his thoughts

instead to the stars what use to him these
parrots mister galileo clears his

vision with chamois discovers sun moon
and their retinue dreams deep like in thought

of night birds and wishes by day he had
plumage the color of stars

                    *

good day mister gutenberg says a vintner from
mainz as he blinks at the master with both eyes

he knows the master prints wisdom from wine-
presses the black and the white of it is

master johannes's business as they climb down
the stairs to the cellar and exchange news ripe

for printing the vintner leaves behind vintnering
he is now the blinking apprentice of gutenberg

am anfang sei der bleisatz meint johann der
winzer nickt macht licht im keller und weiss

was zu tun ist er panscht die schwärze er zapft
das letzte fass im feuchten keller vielfältig

werden die alten weisheiten nun unter dem
druck der presse herr gutenberg sinnt über

schriften nach bleischwer und reif zum druck
sollen sie sein der winzer keltert seite eins

*

ein wenig einsam steht henry ford am eingang
seiner faktorei und harrt der herstellung einzeln

leistet eine sonne hitze am mittag fords module
werden geschraubt wie genietet aus schloten

steigt fabrikgetreu staub und rauch auf henry ford
sieht die motorisierten modelle in alle richtungen

ziehen er winkt einigen leichter hand nach die
wagen gleichen sich in weiter ferne sie stossen

rauch aus wirbeln staub auf henry ford steht ein
wenig verloren vor der sonne und entfernt sorgsam

schmutz wie schweiss aus seinem weissen kragen
in der mittagszeit leistet die sonne einiges sie ruft

bei ford schweiss hervor in der faktorei mehren sich
die wagen in fabrikgetreuer eile sie stehen schlange

to begin there's the lead type says johannes the vintner
nods and lights up the cellar and knows

what to do he dilutes the black taps the last
barrel in the damp cellar and the old

wisdom is now manifold under the pressure
of the press mr gutenberg broods over

texts heavy as lead and be they ripe for printing
the vintner will press the first page

     *

a little bit lonesome henry ford stands at the entrance
to his factory awaiting production the sun alone

the singular heat-source at noon model fords
are bolted and riveted and from the factory smoke-

stacks dust and smoke are rising in factory-fashion
henry ford sees the motorized models proliferating

in every direction he waves a deft hand the cars
resemble themselves on into the distance they belch

forth smoke swirl dust upon henry ford who is standing
a little bit lost under the sun carefully removing

dirt wiping sweat from his white collar at noon
the sun provides much it brings the sweat

forth from ford in the factory the cars increase
they hasten factory-fashion they stand in line

ford flieht die hitze er flitzt in einer seiner tin lizzies
der fahrtwind lockert ihm trocken staub im kragen

    *

indien wenn ich mich nicht irre kichert
columbus er steigt an land die amerikaner

freuen sich ganz uneuropäisch tanzen sie um
die flotte besatzung columbus hält ausschau

nach schaustellern für spanische schaubuden
wo rauch ist in amerika ist auch eine nachricht

des erstaunens die amerikaner versammeln
sich columbus macht einen kleinen schritt

auf sein indien zu die amerikaner einen grossen
richtung manitu wenn sie sich nicht irren sie

kichern wie columbus er schätzt die welt neu ein
wie er ein indien gefunden er kichert und winkt

dutzende tanzende amerikaner an bord flott trinkt
die verdutzte besatzung zu indischem tanz wo

feuerwasser ist ist auch rauch im irren indien die
amerikaner prosten ihrem sehr erhitzten manitu zu

ford flees the heat speeds away in a tin lizzie of his
the air stream working loose the dirt from his collar

*

india if i'm not mistaken snickers columbus
as he climbs ashore the americans

are glad are dancing very uneuropean
around the fleet his crew keeps watch out

for performers for faraway spanish stages
where there's smoke in america there's also a message

of astonishment the americans gather together
columbus takes one small step

toward his india the americans a great leap
toward manitou if they're not mistaken they

snicker like columbus appraising the world anew
like he's found an india he laughs and waves

dozens of dancing americans aboard the baffled
crew frantically drinks to the indian dance where there's fire-

water there's also smoke in this madly mistaken india
the americans raise a toast their manitou madly inflamed.

RM

A NOTE FROM
THE MAX GEILINGER FOUNDATION, ZURICH

The foundation that marks its fiftieth anniversary with the publication of this anthology is named after a man who—a poet himself—was dedicated to cultural exchange through literature.

Though his creative curiosity and aptitude for expressing himself in verse were apparent at an early age, Max Geilinger (1884-1948) initially embarked on the bourgeois career path prescribed by tradition and convention for the scion of an old Zurich family like his own. After finishing his studies in jurisprudence, as well as his law examination, he worked for many years in the state chancellery for the Canton of Zurich, lastly as Deputy Town Secretary. However, he found this work unfulfilling. Finding his material circumstances altered after the death of his father, he quit the civil service in 1930. Thereafter he devoted himself entirely to literary work and, in the years that followed, received ever increasing public recognition. He left behind thirteen volumes of poetry—permanent additions to Switzerland's poetic legacy—eleven dramatic works, two prose volumes, and six books of translated verse, especially from the English.

Max Geilinger's wife, Frances Dalton, a native of England, had seen to it in her will that a Foundation was established, both in order to honor the memory of the poet and to promote the distribution of his works. The Foundation was founded in 1962. Geilinger's life and work were described on behalf of the Foundation in 1967 by Alfred A. Häsler, and published in two volumes.

By way of financial contributions, the Foundation continually fosters literary and cultural relations between Switzerland and the Anglo-Saxon world. Moreover, the Max Geilinger-Preis, with a current monetary award of CHF 25,000, is periodically conferred on individuals or institutions that have enhanced relations between Switzerland and the English-speaking world. Prize recipients have included: in 1972, the Zurich James Joyce scholar Fritz Senn; in 1975, Elisabeth Schnack, Zurich, for providing readers of German access to English-language literature from Ireland, England, Scotland, the USA, Australia, and South Africa; in 1982, William G. Moulton of Princeton University, USA, for linguistic research into Swiss-German dialect; in 1986, James Martin Lindsay of Perth University, Australia, for his work on Gottfried Keller; and in 1988, Christopher Middleton, University of Texas at Austin, USA, for his translations of Robert Walser.

Over time, the Foundation extended its circle of potential prize recipients beyond translation work. These honorees have included: in 1991, Gordon A. Craig, Stanford University in Palo Alto, USA, for his work *Geld und Geist: Zürich im Zeitalter des Liberalismus 1830–1869* (The Triumph of Liberalism: Zurich in the Golden Age, 1830-1869); in 2000, Stephen P. Halbrook, Fairfax, Virginia, USA, for his book *Target Switzerland: Swiss Armed*

Neutrality in World War II; in 2002, the Zurich Comedy Club for its dedication in introducing Anglo-Saxon theatrical productions into the cultural life of Zurich; in 2007, Rüdiger Ahrens, University of Würzburg, Andreas Fischer, University of Zurich, and Ulrich Suerbaum, Ruhr University Bochum, as editors of the English-German study edition of Shakespeare's plays. Since the Foundation's establishment, a total of 16 awards ceremonies have taken place, by means of which the literary and cultural relations between Switzerland and the English-speaking world have been significantly advanced.

On the fiftieth anniversary of its founding, the Foundation presents the public with this anthology of recent Swiss poetry. Just as Max Geilinger once rendered English poetry more available to German-speaking lands, this anniversary volume provides English-speaking readers with poetry from all four Swiss languages. In so doing, the anthology fills a gap. At the same time, it shares the spirit and vocation of the prize-winner in this anniversary year, the Translation House Looren in Wernetshausen in the Zurich Oberland.

Peter Mousson
President of the Foundation
May 8, 2012

THE POETS

VALERIO ABBONDIO (1891–1958). Born in Ascona; died in Mendrisio (Canton Ticino). Educated in Lugano. Studied literature in Fribourg and Milan. French instructor at the higher secondary school in Lugano. His poetry collections include *Betulle* (1922) and *Cerchi d'argento* (1944). He has also produced essays—most of the latter for the journal *Pagine nostre*, published in Lugano.

URS ALLEMANN (1948–). Born in Schlieren (Canton Zurich). Studied German, English, and sociology in Bonn, Berlin, Marburg, and Hannover. Worked as editor of *Theater heute* and feuilleton editor for the *Basler Zeitung*. His published works include the poetry collection *Holder die Polder* (2001), as well as novels such as *Der alte Mann und die Bank* (1993). Lives as a freelance writer in Reigoldswil near Basel. Won the 1991 Preis des Landes Kärnten at the Ingeborg Bachmann Prize for his novel *Babyficker* (1992; *Babyfucker*, 2010), as well as the 2012 Heimrad-Bäcker-Preis.

DUMENIC ANDRY (1960–). Born in Zurich. Raised in Ramosch and Chur. Studied Romance languages at the University of Zurich. Taught at the higher secondary school in Ftan. Lives as a freelance writer, journalist, and translator in Zuoz (Canton Graubünden). Author of poetry and prose in Rhaeto-Romanic, specifically the Vallader dialect, as well as Rumantsch Grischun; his publications include the collection *Uondas: raquints cuorts* (2008). Awarded, among other prizes, the Swiss Schiller Foundation Award 2009.

HANS ARP (1886–1966). Born in Strasbourg; died in Basel. Trained as a painter and sculptor in Weimar and Paris. Connected to the "Blaue Reiter" artist group in Munich. Co-founder of the Dada movement in Zurich. Married to the painter Sophie Taeuber. Lived in Meudon near Paris and in Switzerland. In addition to his work in the visual arts, he wrote poems in German and French. Won a number of important awards for literature and art, including the Grand Prize for Sculpture at the 1954 Venice Biennale.

EMMY BALL-HENNINGS (1885–1948). Born in Flensburg (Germany); died in Sorengo (Canton Ticino). Actress and cabaret artist, emigrated to Switzerland. Co-founder of the Dada movement. Married Hugo Ball in 1920. Published poetry, including her collection *Die letzte Freude* (1913) as well as novels, including *Gefängnis* (1919).

HUGO BALL (1886–1927). Born in Pirmasens (Germany); died in Sant'Abbondio (Canton Ticino). Trained as director and dramaturge with Max Reinhardt in Berlin. Emigrated to Switzerland in 1915. Co-founder of the Cabaret Voltaire; led the Dada movement in Zurich. Married Emmy Hennings in 1920. Author of poetry, essays, plays, a memoir/diary entitled *Die Flucht aus der Zeit* (1927; *Flight out of Time*, 1974), a novel, and a biography of Hermann Hesse entitled *Hermann Hesse: Sein Leben und sein Werk* (1927).

PINO BERNASCONI (1904–1983). Born in Riva San Vitale (Canton Ticino). Studied law in Rome. Had a successful career as lawyer, judge, publisher, and politician in Lugano. Was the editor of various newspapers and journals (*Gazetta Ticinese, Il Dovere*). Author of poetry in the Ticinese dialect, including in his collection *L'üra dübia* (1957).

DONATA BERRA (1947–). Born and raised in Milan, where she studied literature and music. Lecturer at the University of Bern. Published translations of Dürrenmatt, Klaus Merz, and others. A poet, she won the 1993 Swiss Schiller Foundation individual works Prize for her collection *Santi quattro coronati*, as well as the 1997 Literary Award of the Canton Bern.

CLO DURI BEZZOLA (1945–2004). Born and raised in Scuol in the Lower Engadine (Canton Graubünden). Trained as a primary and secondary school teacher in Chur and Zurich. Taught at Sils in the Engadine, and at Oetwil on the Lake of Zurich. Author of poetry, including his collection *Il blau engulà* (1998), as well as prose, novels—including *Zwischenzeit* (1996)—and plays in both German and in Rhaeto-Romanic, specifically the Vallader dialect and (for example, the poem "Limità") in Rumantsch Grischun.

GIOVANNI BIANCONI (1891–1981). Born and died in Minusio (Canton Ticino). Trained at the Arts School in St. Gallen and the Academy of Fine Arts in Stuttgart. Worked as a drawing instructor in Locarno; conducted extensive ethnographic research into the culture of the Ticino region. Struggled for the preservation of rural culture, created numerous woodcuts, and wrote poetry in the Ticinese dialect, for example in his collection *Garbiröö* (1942).

VANNI BIANCONI (1977–). Born in Locarno (Canton Ticino). Studied literature at the University of Milan. Director of the annual literature and translation festival "Babel" in Bellinzona. Currently lives in London, where in addition to his poetry, including his collection *Faura dei morti* (2004), he has produced several translations of English-language literature, including works by W. H. Auden and Somerset Maugham. For his Auden translation he was awarded the Premio Marazza Opera prima.

CORINNA BILLE (1912–1979). Born in Lausanne, grew up in the Valais. Lived in France, Italy, and Spain. Married Maurice Chappaz in 1947. Published poems, novels, and stories. Won the Swiss Schiller Foundation Award in 1974 and the Bourse Goncourt de la nouvelle in 1975 for her story collection *La Demoiselle sauvage*.

NICOLAS BOUVIER (1929–1998). Spent his childhood in Grand-Lancy (Canton Geneva); he later studied law and the humanities at the University of Geneva. Worked as a journalist and photographer. Writer of travelogues, a novel, and poems. Made extensive voyages to Asia, the first of them in a (now legendary) Fiat Topolino, as celebrated in his most famous book, *L'Usage du monde* (1963; *The Way of the World*, 1992). Winner of numerous prizes, including the Prix Rambert (1968), Prix des Belles-Lettres (1986), Prix de la Ville de Genève (1987), and the Grand Prix C. F. Ramuz (1995).

RAINER BRAMBACH (1917–1983). Born the son of a German immigrant in Basel. Drafted into the German Army in 1939. Escaped into Switzerland. Worked as a house painter, gardener, stonemason, and, after 1959, as a writer in Basel. Published both poetry, including *Tagwerk* (1959) and fiction, including *Wahrnehmungen* (1961). Received, among other prizes, the Hugo-Jacobi-Preis in 1955.

AURELIO BULETTI (1946–). Born in Giubiasco (Canton Ticino). Studied in Milan. Taught at the higher secondary school in Lugano. Lives today as a freelance writer in Cassarate. Author of poetry, including the collection *Terzo esile libro di poesie* (1989), as well as prose, including the short-story collection *Trenta racconti brevi* (1984). Winner of the Swiss Schiller Foundation Award in 1984, and the Swiss Schiller Foundation individual works Prize in 2006.

ERIKA BURKART (1922–2010). Born in Aarau. Trained as a primary school teacher. Traveled to France, Spain, Italy, and Ireland. Taught primary school until 1953, then lived as a freelance writer in Aristau (Canton Aargau). Published poetry, including the collections *Der dunkle Vogel* (1953) and *Die Zärtlichkeit der Schatten* (1991), as well as novels, including *Moräne* (1970). A selection of her awards include the Swiss Schiller Foundation individual works Prize (1958 and 1971), the Conrad-Ferdinand-Meyer-Preis (1961), the Gottfried-Keller-Preis (1991), and the Great Schiller Prize of the Swiss Schiller Foundation (2005).

ARTUR CAFLISCH (1893–1971). Born and died in Zuoz in the Upper Engadine (Canton Graubünden). Studied music and literature in Zurich. Taught at Santa Maria in the Müstair Valley and in St. Moritz (Canton Graubünden). Freelance writer in Zuoz from 1936 onward. Published poetry, songs, stories, fables, and aphorisms.

ARNO CAMENISCH (1978–). Born in Tavanasa (Canton Graubünden). Studied at the Swiss Literature Institute in Biel. Writes in Rhaeto-Romantic, German, Bündnerdeutsch, and hybrid forms. He debuted in 2005 with *Ernesto ed autres Manzegnas*, but is best known for his award-winning novels, *Sez Ner* (2009) and *Hinter dem Bahnhof* (2010)—the first two oparts of a widely acclaimed trilogy. With links to the Spoken Word scene in Switzerland, he has recently been publishing poetry in literary magazines and anthologies. In 2010, he was awarded both the ZKB Schillerpreis and the Berner Literaturpreis for *Sez Ner*.

BLAISE CENDRARS (1887–1961). Born in La Chaux-de-Fonds (Canton Neuchâtel) as Frédéric-Louis Sauser. Began his life as an adventurer at age sixteen, interrupted by studies (medicine and philosophy) at the University of Bern: journeys to Russia, Brazil, the USA; participant in the Parisian Avant-Garde (Apollinaire, Chagall, Sonia Delaunay); took part in World War I as a volunteer in the French Foreign Legion. Lived for the rest of his life mainly in Paris. His considerable body of work includes novels (*Moravagine*, 1926; 1968), stories, essays, memoirs (*L'Homme foudroyé*, 1945; *The Astonished Man*, 1970) and poems (*La prose du Transsibérien et de la Petite Jehanne de France*, 1913). In 1961 he was awarded the Grand Prix littéraire de la Ville de Paris.

MAURICE CHAPPAZ (1916–2009). Born in Lausanne. Attended secondary school at the collège of the Abbey of Saint-Maurice. Studied in Lausanne and

Geneva. Lived with his wife Corinna Bille in Veyras (Canton Valais). He published poetry (including *Testament du Haut-Rhône*, 1953), stories, essays, diaries, and polemics. Winner of many literary prizes, including the Prix Rambert (1953), Prix de l'État du Valais (1985), Great Schiller Prize of the Swiss Schiller Foundation (1997), and the Bourse Goncourt de la poésie (1997).

Pierre Chappuis (1930–). Born in Tavannes (Canton Bern). Studied literature in Geneva. Lives in Neuchâtel, where since 1993 he has taught at a higher secondary school. Author of essays and poetry, including the recent collection of poetic prose texts, *Muettes émergences* (2011). Literary awards include the 1997 Swiss Schiller Foundation Award and the 2005 Grand Prix C.F. Ramuz for his complete works.

Jacques Chessex (1934–2009). Born in Payerne; died in Yverdon-les-Bains (Canton Vaud). Studied literature in Lausanne. Lived in Ropraz, where he taught at the higher secondary school. His ample body of work includes novels, stories, essays, and poems. He was the winner of numerous prizes, including the Swiss Schiller Foundation Award (1963), the Prix Alpes-Jura (1971), the Prix Goncourt for his novel *L'Ogre* in 1973 (*A Father's Love*, 1975; *The Tyrant*, 2012), the Bourse Goncourt de la poésie (2004), and the Grand Prix Jean-Giono Lifetime achievement Award from the Swiss Schiller Foundation (2007).

Francesco Chiesa (1871–1973). Born in Sagno (Canton Ticino). Studied law in Pavia, became Secretary for the Public Prosecutor's Office, and then a teacher of literature and art history at the higher secondary school in Lugano, where he was later Principal. Author of poetry, including the collection *Calliope* (1907); stories, including the collection *Tempo di marzo* (1925); and novels, including *Villadorna* (1928). He was awarded the 1927 Great Schiller Prize of the Swiss Schiller Foundation and the Premio Mondadori 1928, as well as honorary doctorates from the Universities of Lausanne, Rome, and Pavia.

Edmond-Henri Crisinel (1897–1948). Born in Faoug (Canton Vaud). Attended school in Murten and Lausanne. Worked as a journalist at the *Revue de Lausanne*. Suffered from frequent bouts of depression and hospital stays; committed suicide in Lake Geneva, near Nyon. Author of poetry, including the collections *Le Veilleur* (1939), *Alectone* (1944), and *Nuit de juin* (1945), as well as prose. His collected poetry was published in 1949; his collected works were published in 1979.

FRANÇOIS DEBLUË (1950–). Born in Pully (Canton Vaud). Studied literature in Lausanne. Taught higher secondary school in Lausanne and at the University of Lausanne. Author of poems, prose, essays, and works for the stage. Won the Prix Yves-Chammah for his poetry collection *Travail de temps* in 1986, the Prix Michel-Dentan for his novella *Troubles fêtes* in 1990, the Swiss Schiller Foundation individual works Prize for his mixed collection of prose and poetry *Figures de la patience* in 1999, and a second Schiller Award for his entire œuvre in 2004.

SYLVIANE DUPUIS (1956–). Born in Geneva. Studied literature and archeology in Geneva, where she teaches at a higher secondary school and at the University. She has traveled to Greece, Turkey, China, and Africa. Author of poetry, including the collections *D'un lieu l'autre* (1985) and *Géométrie de l'illimité* (2000), as well as plays and essays. Won the Prix C. F. Ramuz (1986), the Prix international francophone de poésie (1996), the Prix des Journées de Lyon des Auteurs de théâtre (2004), and the Prix Pittard de l'Andelyn (2012).

ADELHEID DUVANEL (1936–1996). Born in Basel. Trained as a textile-illustrator at the Arts School there. Suffered from acute depression, and froze to death after taking sleeping pills in the woods near Basel. Author of poetry and prose; primarily known for her very short, often nightmarish stories, as appeared in such collections as *Das Brillenmuseum* (1982) and *Das verschwundene Haus* (1985). Recipient of the 1981 Kleiner Basler Kunstpreis, the 1984 Kranichsteiner Literaturpreis, and the Swiss Schiller Award for her entire œuvre in 1988.

LUISA FAMOS (1930–1974). Born and reared in Ramosch in the Lower Engadine (Canton Graubünden). A primary school teacher in the Engadine and in Canton Zurich. Contributor to Romanish radio and television. Spent many years in Honduras and Venezuela. Her poetic œuvre—much of it published posthumously—is small but influential. Won the 1961 Swiss Schiller Foundation individual works Prize for her collection *Mumaints*.

REMO FASANI (1922–2011). Born in Mesocco (Canton Graubünden). Studied linguistics and literature in Zurich and Florence. Higher secondary school teacher in Chur, professor of Italian Language and Literature at the University of Neuchâtel. Has published works of literary criticism and poetry, including the collections *Senso dell'esilio: Poesie 1944–1945* (1945) and *Oggi come oggi* (1976), as well as translations of poetry from German.

Three-time winner of the Swiss Schiller Foundation Award, in 1975, 1983, and 2000, as well as the Bündner Kulturpreis in 1994.

CLAIRE GENOUX (1971–). Born in Lausanne. Studied literature in Lausanne. Teaches at the Swiss Literature Institute in Biel. Author of poetry and short fiction. Won the Prix de poésie C. F. Ramuz for *Saisons du corps* (1999). Her *Poésie 1997–2004* was published in 2010 and her recent collection *Faire feu* in 2011.

EUGEN GOMRINGER (1925–). Born in Cachuela Esperanza (Bolivia). Studied in Bern and Rome (political economy and art history). Professor of Aesthetics at the National Academy of Art, Düsseldorf. In 2000, he founded in Rehau (Germany), his current place of residence, the Institute for Constructive Art and Concrete Poetry. Author of essays and poems in various languages. Has won numerous prizes, including the Kulturpreis der Stadt Rehau in 1997, and the Premio Punta Tragara per la Poesia Concreta in 2007.

ALEXANDER XAVER GWERDER (1923–1952). Born in Thalwil (Canton Zurich). Apprenticed as an offset-copyist and worked in this profession, while writing poetry, short fiction, and essays. Committed suicide in Arles in Southern France. His collected works and selected letters were published in 1998.

ROLF HERMANN (1973–). Born in Sierre (Canton Valais). Studied English and German in Fribourg, Bern, and Iowa, USA. Lives and works in Biel. In addition to his poetry, including the collections *Hommage an das Rückenschwimmen in der Nähe von Chicago und anderswo* (2007) and *Kurze Chronik einer Bruchlandung* (2011), he writes prose, radio plays, stage plays, and texts for performance. Winner of the Advancement Award of the Canton Valais in 2009 and the Tübinger Stadtschreiberstipendium für Lyrik in 2010.

VIC HENDRY (1920–). Born in Tujetsch/Cavorgia (Canton Graubünden). Trained at the teachers college in Chur and at the Universities of Fribourg and Zurich. Worked as a secondary school teacher in Schaffhausen. Lives in Schaffhausen. Author of poems, prose, biographies, historical treatises, radio plays, and educational radio programs. Won the 1992 Schiller Award for his entire œuvre as well as the 2001 Culture Prize of the Canton Graubünden.

Felix Philipp Ingold (1942–). Born in Basel. Studied Slavic languages and comparative literature in Basel and Paris. Research appointment and work in Eastern Europe. Works as a cultural commentator, translator, and anthologist, and was a professor of Russian cultural history at the University of St. Gallen from 1971 to 2005. Lives in Zurich and Romainmôtier. Author of novels and essays in addition to his poetry, which has been collected in such volumes as *Schwarz auf Schnee* (1967) and *Tagesform* (2007). Winner of numerous prizes, including the 1989 Petrarca-Prize for literary translation, the Literary Award of the Canton Bern in 1998, the Ernst-Jandl-Preis in 2003, the Erlanger Literary Award for Poetry and Translation in 2005, and the Lyrik Award Basel in 2009.

Philippe Jaccottet (1925–). Born in Moudon (Canton Vaud). Studied literature in Lausanne. Has lived in Grignan (France) since 1953. Is as well known as a translator as he is as a poet, prose writer, and essayist, having translated into French, among other authors: Homer, Robert Musil, Leopardi, Ungaretti, Hölderlin, Rilke, Góngora and Mandelstam. Several of his poetry collections have been translated into English, including, most recently, *And, Nonetheless: Selected Prose and Poetry 1990–2009* (2011). Winner of numerous prizes, including the Grand Prix C.F. Ramuz (1970), the Prix Montaigne (1972), the Bourse Goncourt de la poésie (2003), and the Great Schiller Prize of the Swiss Schiller Foundation (2010). His collected poems are forthcoming in a Gallimard-Pléiade edition, a rare honor for a living author.

Adolfo Jenni (1911–1997). Born in Modena (Italy); died in Muri (Canton Bern). Studied literature in Parma and Bologna. Worked as a lecturer, then Professor of Italian Literature at the University of Bern. In addition to poetry (including the collections *Foglie* [1938], *Recitativi* [1971], and *Le quattro stagioni* [1973]), he was also the author of essays and literary criticism. Twice, in 1937 and 1942, he won the Swiss Schiller Foundation Award.

Göri Klainguti (1945–). Born in Pontresina in the Upper Engadine (Canton Graubünden). Trained as a secondary school teacher in Zurich. Lives as a farmer, sculptor, painter, and writer in Samedan. Author of poetry in the Puter dialect, as well as plays, stories (e.g., *Gian Sulvèr*, 1977), and novels (e.g., *Lü* 2005). Winner, among other prizes, of Schiller Award for his entire œuvre in 2005.

PEIDER LANSEL (1863–1943). Born in Pisa; died in Geneva. Worked in the family business in Tuscany. Lived in Livorno, Geneva, and Sent (Lower Engadine, Canton Graubünden). Struggled for the preservation of the *quarta lingua*. Researched and collected Rhaeto-Romanic cultural artifacts and edited numerous poetry anthologies. Author of poems, essays, and polemics. Received an honorary doctorate from the University of Zurich in 1933, and the Great Schiller Prize of the Swiss Schiller Foundation in 1943. His collected works were published in 2012.

BERNADETTE LERJEN-SARBACH (1942–). Born in Visp (Canton Valais). Trained as a kindergarten teacher. Lives in Zizers (Canton Graubünden). Author of poetry, collected in such volumes as *Ich ha mi geschter im Schaufenschter gsee* (1992), as well as prose, both written in the dialect of the Valais as well as German. Several of her poems were set to music by the Swiss composer Heinz Holliger. Awarded, among other prizes, the Bündner Literaturpreis of the Milly Enderlin Foundation in 2003.

ALEXANDER LOZZA (1880–1953). Born in Marmorera; died in Tiefenkastel (Canton Graubünden). Trained as a Catholic priest in Genoa. Worked as a translator, as well as producing poetry, short fiction, and essays in the infrequently published Rhaeto-Romanic dialect of Surmiran.

PIETRO DE MARCHI (1958–). Born in Seregno (Italy). Studied literature in Milan. Has lived in Zurich since 1984. Teaches Italian literature at the universities of Zurich and Neuchâtel. Writes poems and essays. Won the 2007 Schiller Prize for his poetry collection *Replica*. Co-founder of a study group at the University of Zurich investigating the poetry of quadrilingual Switzerland and its translation.

KURT MARTI (1921–). Born in Bern. Studied theology in Bern and Basel. Worked as a prison chaplain in Paris and a minister in Leimiswil, Niederlenz, and in Bern. Author of poetry in standard German and in dialect, as well as short fiction, a novel, cultural criticism, and theological writings. His collected works to date were published in 1996, and his most recent poetry collection, *Zoé Zebra*, was published in 2004. Winner of numerous prizes, including the Johann-Peter-Hebel-Preis (1972), the Literary Award of the Canton Bern (1972), and the Swiss Schiller Foundation Award (1986 and 2011). He holds an honorary doctorate from the University of Bern (1977).

GRYTZKO MASCIONI (1936–2003). Born in Villa di Tirano (Italy); died in Nice (France). Grew up in the Valtellina Valley, Puschlav, and Engadine. Studied law in Milan. Was co-founder of the Italophone Swiss-Italian television network Radio Svizzera as well as Director of the Italian Institute in Zagreb. Author of poetry, including the collections *Il favoloso spreco* (1968) and *I passeri di Horkheimer e Transeuropa* (1969), as well as short fiction, novels, and essays. Among numerous other awards, he won the Premio Amalfi in 1967 and the Schiller Award for his entire œuvre in 2000.

PIERRE-LOUIS MATTHEY (1893–1970). Born in Avenex-sur-Nyon (Canton Vaud); died in Geneva. Son of a pastor. Lived until 1940 in Paris as a dandy and a poet of, at that time, "forbidden" passions, after which he returned to Geneva. Won the Prix Rambert in 1947, the Schiller Award in 1954 and 1969, and the Grand Prix C.F. Ramuz in 1955. A four-volume critical edition of his collected writings, as well as a fifth volume devoted to his translations of English poets, are forthcoming from the Centre de recherches sur les lettres romandes.

NIKLAUS MEIENBERG (1940–1993). Born in St. Gallen. Committed suicide in Zurich. Studied history in Fribourg. Worked as journalist. Wrote socio-critical journalism about historical and contemporary Switzerland, as well as poetry, for example in his collections *Die Erweiterung der Pupillen beim Eintritt ins Hochgebirge: Poesie 1966–1981* (1981) and *Geschichte der Liebe und des Liebäugelns* (1993). Won, among other awards, a Grant from the Max-Frisch-Foundation (1988), and the Culture Prize of the City of St. Gallen (1990).

GERHARD MEIER (1917–2008). Born in Niederbipp (Canton Bern). Abandoned engineering studies and worked in a lamp factory. From 1957 onward wrote poems, lyrical prose, and novels, including *Toteninsel* (1979; *Isle of the Dead*, 2011). Worked as a freelance writer after 1971. Lived his whole life in Niederbipp, yet associated with many others of his well-known literary contemporaries. Honored with the Petrarca-Prize in 1983, the Hermann-Hesse-Literaturpreis in 1991, the Gottfried-Keller-Preis in 1994, and the Heinrich-Böll-Preis in 1999.

FELICE MENGHINI (1909–1947). Born in Poschiavo (Canton Graubünden), died in an accident in the mountains. Trained as a Catholic priest in Milan, Monza, and Chur. Lived for the most part in Poschiavo. A priest, poet, editor, and translator, his poems appeared in such collections as *Umili cose* (1938) and *Parabola e altre poesie* (1943).

KLAUS MERZ (1945–). Born in Aarau. Trained as a secondary school teacher. Taught language and cultural studies in a polytechnical college. Lives as a freelance writer in Unterkulm (Canton Aargau). Author of poetry, such as collected in *Geschiebe mein Land* (1969) and *Kurze Durchsage* (1995), as well as short fiction, plays, novels, and essays. A frequent collaborator with visual artists. Winner of the Swiss Schiller Foundation Award in both 1979 and 2005, as well as the Hermann-Hesse-Literaturpreis in 1997, the Prix littéraire Lipp Zurich in 1999, the Gottfried-Keller-Preis in 2004, and the Friedrich-Hölderlin-Preis in 2012.

ELISABETH MEYLAN (1937–). Born in Basel, where she studied German and Romance languages. Worked as teacher, lecturer, and editor. Has lived since 1987 as a freelance writer in her home town. Author of poetry, including the collections *Entwurf zu einer Ebene* (1973) and *Die allernächsten Dinge* (1994), as well as prose. Her awards include the Swiss Schiller Foundation Award in 1976.

ALBERTO NESSI (1940–). Born in Mendrisio (Canton Ticino). Reared in Chiasso, where—after training at the teachers college in Locarno and at the University of Fribourg—he taught Italian literature at higher secondary school. Lives as a freelance writer and journalist in the Mendrisiotto. Author of poetry, including the collections *Ai margini* (1973) and *Ode di gennaio* (2005), as well as short fiction and essays. Winner of the Swiss Schiller Foundation Award three times (1976, 1983, and 1986), as well as the Prix littéraire Lipp Zurich in 2003.

GIORGIO ORELLI (1921–). Born in Airolo (Canton Ticino). Studied literature at the University of Fribourg. Taught at a commercial college in Bellinzona. Lives as a freelance writer. Author of poetry, short fiction, and essays, and has published translations of poems by Goethe and Andri Peer. Winner of numerous prizes, including the Premio di poesia of the city of Florence in 1961, the Swiss Schiller Foundation Award for his entire œuvre in 1974, the Great Schiller Prize of the Swiss Schiller Foundation in 1988, and the Premio Bagutta 2002 for his collection *Il collo dell'anitra* (2001).

GIOVANNI ORELLI (1928–). Born in Bedretto (Canton Ticino). Trained at the teachers college in Locarno and at the universities of Milan and Zurich. Taught at higher secondary school in Lugano and worked for Swiss-Italian radio and television. Author of novels, stories, and poems in both standard Italian and Ticinese dialect, including the novel *Il sogno di Walacek* (1991;

Walaschek's Dream, 2012). Among his many awards are the Prix Veillon (1964), the Premio l'Inedito Milano (1978), the Gottfried-Keller-Preis Zurich (1997), and the Premio internazionale Dei due laghi Como-Lugano (1995).

ANDRI PEER (1921–1985). Born in Sent (Canton Graubünden). Spent his childhood in the Lower Engadine (Sent, Carolina, Lavin). Trained at the teachers college in Chur and at the Universities of Zurich and Paris. Taught at the higher secondary school in Winterthur and at the University of Zurich. Has worked as an editor, journalist, and translator. Author of poetry, debuting with the collection *La trais-cha dal temp* in 1946, as well as short fiction, essays, radio plays, and stage plays. His awards include the Premio Cortina di poesia della montagna (1978) and the Premio Ascona per la narrative (1985).

ANNE PERRIER (1922–). Born in Lausanne. Studied at the University of Lausanne. Traveled to Greece. Writes mainly poems. Her *Poésie 1960–1986* was published in 1988. Won the prestigious French Grand Prix national de poésie in 2012. Previous recognitions include the Prix Rambert in 1971 and the Prix vaudois des écrivains in 1996.

RUT PLOUDA (1948–). Born in Tarasp in the Lower Engadine (Canton Graubünden). Primary school teacher in Savognin and Ftan. Lives in Ftan. Author of poetry, including the collection *Föglias aint il vent*, as well as short fiction and a novel. Winner of the UBS Jubilee Fund Award in 1994 and 2001, as well the Swiss Schiller Foundation Award in 2001 and the Bündner Literaturpreis der Stiftung Milly Enderlin in 2001.

FABIO PUSTERLA (1957–). Born in Mendrisio (Canton Ticino). Studied at the University of Pavia. Taught at the higher secondary school in Lugano. Author of poetry, including the collections *Le cose senza storia* (1994) and *Cocci e frammenti* (2011), as well as essays and translations. Honored with numerous prizes: the Swiss Schiller Foundation individual works Prize (1986, 2000, 2011), the Premio Montale (1986), the Premio Prezzolini (1994), the Premio Hermann Ganz (1995), and the Premio Metauro (1995).

ANTONIO ROSSI (1952–). Born in Maroggia (Canton Ticino). Studied literature in Fribourg and Florence. Taught at the higher secondary school in Mendrisio. Author of poetry, including the collections *Ricognizioni* (1979), *Glyphé* (1989), and *Sesterno* (2005), as well as essays and translations. Winner of the Swiss Schiller Foundation Award in 1980, the Premio Lorenzo Montano in 1996, and the Premio Sertoli Salis in 2006.

GUSTAVE ROUD (1897–1976). Born in Saint-Légier (Canton Vaud). Studied literature in Lausanne. Lived as freelance writer on the family estate in Carrouge. Author of poetry, lyrical prose, essays, and translations (Hölderlin, Trakl, Gotthelf). His three-volume collected writings, *Écrits I, II, III*, were first published in 1978. Awarded, among other prizes, the Prix Rambert (1941) and the Prix de la Ville de Lausanne (1967). In 1957 he was given an honorary doctorate from the University of Lausanne.

ELIO SCAMARA (1930–2011). Born in Lavertazza (Canton Ticino). Worked as a bus driver. Has published two volumes of poetry in the Ticinese dialect: *El nono et fràssenn* (1990) and *Er mágn* (1995). Won the Premio di poesia "Città di Legnano Giuseppe Tirinnanzi" in 1992.

LETA SEMADENI (1944–). Born in Scuol (Canton Graubünden). Studied in Zurich. Contributor to radio and television. Lives in Lavin in the Lower Engadine. Primarily a poet, in the Vallader dialect as well as in German. Her collections include *Poesias da chadafö* (2006) and *In mia vita da vuolp* (2010). She won the Swiss Schiller Foundation Award and the Bündner Literaturpreis, both in 2011.

ARMIN SENSER (1964–). Born in Biel (Canton Bern). Studied philosophy in Bern. Lives in Berlin. His poetry collections include *Grosses Erwachen* (1999) and *Kalte Kriege* (2007), and he is also the author of plays and essays. Prizes won include the Lyrik-Debüt-Preis (1999), the Book Prize from the City of Bern (1999), and the H. C. Artmann Literaturpreis der Stadt Salzburg (2009).

HENDRI SPESCHA (1928–1982). Born in Trun (Canton Graubünden). Studied in Zurich and Fribourg. Lived in Domat/Ems. Worked as a secondary school teacher and Secretary of the Lia Rumantscha, an organization that promotes Rhaeto-Romanic language and culture. A contributor to Rhaeto-Romanic television. Published several volumes of poetry, including *Sinzurs* (1958), *Sendas* (1975), and *Per tei e per mei* (1983), as well as stories and radio plays. Won the Swiss Schiller Foundation Award in 1964.

ALBERT STREICH (1897–1960). Born in Brienz; died in Interlaken (Canton Bern). Lived in Brienz. Worked as a laborer, constable, and in the Brienz city hall. In addition to his poetry, he produced tales and other short fiction in dialect and in standard German. His complete works were published in three volumes between 1970 and 1980. Won the 1946 Literary Award of the Canton Bern and the 1957 Literature Prize of the City of Bern.

PIERRE-ALAIN TÂCHE (1940–). Born in Lausanne. Studied law in Lausanne. Worked as a lawyer and judge in Lausanne, as well as in various cultural institutions. Producing poetry exclusively, his recent books include *L'air des hautbois: variations sur la Folia* (2010) and *Dernier état des lieux* (2011). Prizes awarded: the Swiss Schiller Foundation Award (1975, 1984), the Grand Prix du Mont-Saint-Michel (1991), and the Prix Roger-Kowalski (2011).

JOSÉ-FLORE TAPPY (1954–). Born in Lausanne. Studied literature in Lausanne. Works as a literary scholar. Author of five volumes of poetry, including *Terre battue* (1995) and *Lunaires* (2001). Has also produced essays and co-translations with Marion Graf (of Erika Burkart and Anna Akhmatova), as well as edited editions of other poets' work (Jaccottet). Numerous awards include: the Prix C.F. Ramuz for her collection *Errer mortelle* (1983) and the Swiss Schiller Foundation Award individual works Prize for *Hangars* (2006) as well as her entire poetic œuvre.

REGINA ULLMANN (1884–1961). Born in St. Gallen; died in Ebersberg (Germany). Daughter of a German and an Austrian. Lived from 1902–1938 in Munich, where she associated with Rainer Maria Rilke, and from 1938 on in St. Gallen. Author of poetry, but, above all, short fiction, including the collections *Von der Erde des Lebens* (1910), which appeared with a preface by Rilke, and *Die Landstrasse* (1921). In 1954 she received the Kulturpreis der Stadt St. Gallen.

RAPHAEL URWEIDER (1974–). Born in Bern. Studied German and philosophy in Fribourg. Lives in Bern. Works as a musician, rapper, theater-director, and artistic director. Author of poetry, including the collections *Guten Tag Herr Gutenberg* (1999) and *Alle deine Namen* (2008), as well as plays and opera libretti. Has won, among other prizes, the Leonce-and Lena-Prize in 1999, the Swiss Schiller Foundation Award Prize in 2000, and the 2004 Clemens-Brentano-Prize.

PIERRE VOÉLIN (1949–). Born in Courgenay (Canton Jura). Spend his childhood in Porrentruy. Studied art history in Geneva and Fribourg, where he also taught. Lives in Nyon (Canton Vaud). His most recent books are the poetry collection *L'été sans visage* (2010) and the essay collection *De l'air volé* (2012). Received, among other prizes, the Prix Canada-Suisse in 1985 and, in 2004, the Prix de la Commission de littérature de langue française du Canton de Berne for *La nuit accoutumée* (2002) as well as for his entire œuvre.

ROBERT WALSER (1878–1956). Born in Biel (Canton Bern); died in Herisau (Canton Appenzell). Worked as an apprentice at the Bernische Kantonalbank in Biel and then as a freelance writer in Berlin. Lived from 1929 on in a mental institution. Author of poetry, prose pieces, short fiction, novels, mini-dramas, all of which has had tremendous impact on twentieth-century literature, and much of which is now available in English translation.

SILJA WALTER (1919–2011). Born in Rickenbach (Canton Lucerne). Studied literature in Fribourg. Lived from 1948 until her death as a Benedictine nun in the Fahr Abbey near Zurich. Author of poetry, including her debut collection *Die ersten Gedichte* in 1944 and *Die Feuertaube* in 1985, as well as plays and many volumes of short fiction. Winner of the Swiss Schiller Foundation Award Prize in both 1956 and 1992, the Literaturpreis der Stadt Bern in 1967, and the Kunstpreis des Kanton Solothurn in 1971.

FRÉDÉRIC WANDELÈRE (1949–). Born in Fribourg. Studied literature in Geneva. Lives in Fribourg. His most recent books of poetry are *La Compagnie capricieuse* (2012) and *Hilfe fürs Unkraut* (2012), a bilingual volume of selected poems published in Germany. He has also published essays and translations. Winner of the the Bourse du Centre international de poésie, Marseille, in 1991.

ALBIN ZOLLINGER (1895–1941). Born in Zurich. Childhood in Argentina and Switzerland. Attended teachers college. Worked as primary school teacher, journalist, and freelance writer. He published several novels during his lifetime as well as four collections of poetry, including *Sternfrühe* (1936) and *Haus des Lebens* (1939).

GIUSEPPE ZOPPI (1896–1952). Born in Broglio; died in Locarno (Canton Ticino). Studied literature in Fribourg. Taught at higher secondary school in Locarno, and then as Professor of Italian Literature at the Federal Technical University in Zurich (ETH Zurich). In addition to his poetry collections, including *Poesie d'oggi e di ieri* (1944) and *Le alpi* (1957), he published short stories and a novel (*Dove nascono i fiumi*, 1949), as well as translations of, among others, C. F. Meyer and C. F. Ramuz.

THE TRANSLATORS

SIMON KNIGHT lives partly in the UK and partly in Italy, and has a particular interest in Swiss-Italian literature. His translation of Fabio Pusterla's poetry, *Days Full of Caves & Tigers*, appeared from Arc Publications in 2012.

REINHARD MAYER is the author of a study of Thomas Mann, *Fremdlinge im eigenen Haus*, and has published numerous translations and articles in scholarly journals. He has taught at Bennington, Skidmore, and Wheaton Colleges, as well as the University of Illinois at Urbana-Champaign, and has served as a Visiting Professor at NYU.

DONAL MCLAUGHLIN was born in 1961 in Derry, Ireland, and has resided in Scotland since 1970. His short story collection, *an allergic reaction to national anthems & other stories* (2009), was longlisted for the Frank O'Connor Short Story Award and nominated for the EIBF Readers' Best First Book Award. He is a recipient of the Robert Louis Stevenson Memorial Award, was Scottish PEN's first *écrivain sans frontières*, and is a former Hawthornden Fellow. He translated over one hundred writers for the *New Swiss Writing* anthologies (2008–2011) and specializes in translating German-Swiss fiction (Arno Camenisch, Pedro Lenz, Christoph Simon, Urs Widmer).

BURTON PIKE is Professor Emeritus of Comparative Literature and German at the CUNY Graduate Center. He has also taught at the University of Hamburg, Cornell, Queens, and Hunter Colleges of CUNY, and been a Visiting Professor at Yale. He has received a Guggenheim Fellowship and the Medaille für Verdienste um Robert Musil from the City of Klagenfurt. He is a member of the PEN Translation Committee. He edited and co-translated Robert Musil's *The Man without Qualities*, among other works by Musil, and has also translated and written the introductions to Goethe's novel *The Sorrows of Young Werther*, Rilke's novel *The Notebooks of Malte Laurids Brigge*, and most recently Gerhard Meier's novel *Isle of the Dead*, for which he won the 2012 Wolff Translator's Prize.

JAMIE RICHARDS's translations include Nicolai Lilin's *Free Fall*, Serena Vitale's *Shklovsky: Witness to an Era*, Giancarlo Pastore's *Jellyfish*, and Giovanni Orelli's *Walaschek's Dream,* as well as short works by Ermanno Cavazzoni, Igort, and Giacomo Leopardi, among others.

JOHN TAYLOR is the author of the three-volume *Paths to Contemporary French Literature* and *Into the Heart of European Poetry.* He has also written six books of stories, short prose, and poetry, including *The Apocalypse Tapestries* and *If Night Is Falling.* In addition to recent collections of the poetry and prose of Philippe Jaccottet, Jacques Dupin, and Pierre-Albert Jourdan, he has also translated work by Laurence Werner David, Louis Calaferte, Georges Perros, José-Flore Tappy, and Catherine Colomb. He lives in France.

LAUREN K. WOLFE has studied literature and writing at Grinnell College and the School of the Art Institute of Chicago; her translation of Werner Kofler's novel *Am Schreibtisch* is forthcoming from Dalkey Archive Press.

INDEX OF AUTHORS

RIGHTS AND PERMISSIONS

Clo Duri Bezzola: "Limità," from *Il blau engulà / Das gestohlene Blau*, Pendo Verlag, Zurich & Munich, 1998 © Gertrud Bezzola.

Giovanni Bianconi: "Final," from *Garbiröö*, Romerio, Locarno, 1942; "Ricòvar," from *Ofell dal specc*, self-published, Minusio, 1944; "Al sicor cürad föra di strasc," from *Ün güst da pan da segra*, A. Dadò, Locarno, 1986 © Sandro Bianconi.

Vanni Bianconi: "La città senza assedio (*estratti*)," from *Ora prima*, Casagrande, Bellinzona, 2008 © Vanni Bianconi.

Corinna Bille: "Les raisins de verre" and "L'œil sulfate," from *Cent petites histoires cruelles*, Éditions Bertil Galland, Lausanne, 1973 © Fondation de l'Abbaye, Le Châble.

Nicolas Bouvier: "Love Song I," "Love Song II," and "Love Song III," from *Le Dehors et le dedans*, Éditions Zoé, Carouge, 1997 © Éditions Zoé.

Rainer Brambach: "Altersheim" and "Alleinstehende Männer," from *Heiterkeit im Garten. Das gesamte Werk*, Diogenes Verlag, Zurich, 1989 © Diogenes Verlag.

Aurelio Buletti: "Stamani . . ." and "Un lieve segno," from *Né al primo né al più bello*, Iniziative culturali, Sassari, 1979; "Bar Monti," "28.2.," "Poesia spiccia," and "Rivalità," from *E la fragile vita sta nel crucchio*, alla chiara fonte editore, Lugano, 2005 © Aurelio Buletti.

Erika Burkart: "Die Toten," from *Das Licht im Kahlschlag*, Artemis Verlag, Zurich & Stuttgart, 1977 © Ernst Halter.

Artur Caflisch: "Il zurplin" and "In üna pinta," from *Mia Musa*, self-published, Zuoz, 1961 © the estate of Artur Caflisch.

Arno Camenisch: "il tat ha ina vacca . . . ," "negin che capescha . . . ," "la zoppa ei morta . . . ," and "hai semiau," in *Zwischen den Zeilen* 29, November 2008, Urs Engeler Editor © Arno Camenisch.

Blaise Cendrars: "Journal," "Les grands fétiches," and "Construction," from *Du monde entier. Poésies complètes 1912–1924*, Gallimard, Paris 1967. *Journal* et *Construction* issu de *Dix neuf poèmes élastiques.* © 1947, 1963, 2001, 2005 by Éditions Denoël, Paris, and © 1961 by Miriam Cendrars. From vol. 1 of *Tout autour d'aujourd'hui,* Nouvelle édition des œuvres complètes de Blaise Cendrars dirigée par Claude Leroy. *Les grands fétiches* issu de *Poèmes nègres* © Denoël, 1947, 1963, 2001, 2005.

MAURICE CHAPPAZ: "Le Valais au gosier de grive *(extraits),*" from *Le Valais au gosier de grive,* Fata Morgana, Montpellier, 2008 © Fondation de l'Abbaye, Le Châble.

PIERRE CHAPPUIS: "Pleines marges *(extraits),*" from *Pleines marges,* Librairie José Corti, Paris, 1997 © Librairie José Corti.

JACQUES CHESSEX: "Le beau canal," from *Élégie soleil du regret,* Éditions Bertil Galland, Vevey, 1976. "En ce temps-là," from *Les Élégies de Yorick,* Bernard Campiche Éditeur, Yvonand, 1994 © Jean Chessex.

FRANCESCO CHIESA: "Fuochi di primavera," from *Fuochi di primavera,* A.F. Formiggini, Rome, 1919; "Sole di primavera . . . ," from *La stellata sera,* Mondadori, Milan, 1933 © Daniela de Haller-Chiesa.

EDMOND-HENRI CRISINEL: "Élégie de la maison des morts," from *Œuvres,* Éditions L'Âge d'homme, Lausanne, 1979 © Éditions L'Âge d'homme.

FRANÇOIS DEBLUË: "Patience d'un éclair," "Patience d'un homme assoiffé," "Passion de l'homme bafoué," and "Patience de l'homme mendiant," from *Figures de la patience,* Éditions Empreintes, Lausanne, 1998 © François Deblüë. The titles of three poems here published were altered slightly by the author for this edition.

PIETRO DE MARCHI: "Le rose dell'eros," "Asimmetrie," and "Ancora verso Marina," from *Replica,* Casagrande, Bellinzona, 2006; "La catòrbola," from *Parabole smorzate,* Casagrande, Bellinzona, 1999 © Pietro de Marchi.

SYLVIANE DUPUIS: "Emblèmes *(extraits),*" from *Odes brèves,* Éditions Empreintes, Moudon, 1995 © Sylviane Dupuis.

ADELHEID DUVANEL: "Wind" and "Flucht," from *Der letzte Frühlingstag,* Luchterhand Literaturverlag, Munich, 1997.

Luisa Famos: "Il rudè," "Gonda," and "Plövgia," from *Mumaints*, self-published, Cuoira, 1960; "Lügl a Ramosch" and "L'anguel cullas alas d'or," from *Inscunters*, Stamparia Bischofberger, Cuoira, 1974 © Florio Puenter.

Remo Fasani: "Il fiume," from *Qui e ora*, Edizioni Pantarei, Lugano, 1971 © Remo Fasani.

Claire Genoux: "Hiver" and "Étranglement," from *Faire feu*, Bernard Campiche Éditeur, Orbe, 2011 © Bernard Campiche Éditeur.

Eugen Gomringer: "vielleicht," "schweigen schweigen schweigen . . . ," and "schwiizer," from *Vom Rand nach Innen. Die Konstellationen 1951–1995*, Edition Splitter, Vienna, 1995 © Eugen Gomringer.

Alexander Xaver Gwerder: "Damals" and "Ich geh unter lauter Schatten," from *Gesammelte Werke*, Bd. I, Limmat Verlag, Zurich, 1998 © Limmat Verlag.

Vic Hendry: "zacu inagada . . . ," "anemona alva . . . ," "grischa e lonzia . . . ," and "guilas melnas crodan . . . ," from *anemona alva*, Edition Signathur, Dozwil, 2007 © Vic Hendry.

Rolf Hermann: "Hommage an das Rückenschwimmen in der Nähe von Chicago und anderswo," from *Hommage an das Rückenschwimmen in der Nähe von Chicago und anderswo*, Verlag X-Time, Bern, 2007. © Verlag X-Time.

Felix Philipp Ingold: "Himmelskunde" and "Wetterkarte," from *Echtzeit*, Hanser Verlag, Munich & Vienna, 1989 © Felix Philipp Ingold.

Philippe Jaccottet: "Les Pivoines," from *Après beaucoup d'années*, Éditions Gallimard, Paris, 1994 © Éditions Gallimard. John Taylor's 2011 translation, "The Peonies," was first published in Philippe Jaccottet, *And, Nonetheless: Selected Prose and Poetry 1990–2009*, Chelsea Editions, New York, 2011 © John Taylor.

Adolfo Jenni: "Ragazza di paese," from *Poesie e quasi poesie*, Casagrande, Bellinzona, 1987. © Giovanna Jenni.

Göri Klainguti: "Experimaint cun moleküls da H_2O," from *Sprincals*, self-published, Zuoz, 1979 © Göri Klainguti.

PEIDER LANSEL: "Fossas a l'ester" and "Tamangur," from *Poesias originalas e Versiuns poeticas,* Uniun dals Grischs, Sent, and Lia Rumantscha, Chur, 1966 © Uniun dals Grischs and Lia Rumantscha.

BERNADETTE LERJEN-SARBACH: "Gränzä" (see introduction), "Vilicht," "Müet zum Eigenu," and "Bim Schriibu," from *Ich ha mi geschter im Schaufenschter gsee,* Sauerländer Verlag, Aarau, 1992 © Bernadette Lerjen-Sarbach.

ALEXANDER LOZZA: "Return" from *Poesias,* self-published, Chur, 1954 © Duri Loza.

KURT MARTI: "dem herrn unserem gott . . . ," from *Leichenreden,* Luchterhand Verlag, Neuwied & Berlin, 1969; "hommage à rabelais," "wie geits?," and "wo chiemte mer hi?" from *Rosa Loui,* Luchterhand Verlag, Neuwied & Berlin, 1967; "z.b. 25.11.72," from *undereinisch,* Luchterhand Verlag, Neuwied & Berlin, 1973 © Kurt Marti.

GRYTZKO MASCIONI: "Lanceolate aghiformi," "Scusa il disturbo," and "Parlare dei paesi," from *Poesia (1952–1982),* Rusconi, Milan, 1984 © Angela Mascioni Buogo.

PIERRE-LOUIS MATTHEY: "Sonate de l'indigne aveu," from *Œuvres complètes,* Éditions Empreintes, Chavannes-près-Renens, 2013 © Florence Rivier.

NIKLAUS MEIENBERG: "Elegie über den Zufall der Geburt," from *Die Erweiterung der Pupillen beim Eintritt ins Hochgebirge. Poesie 1966–1981,* Limmat Verlag, Zurich, 1981 © Limmat Verlag.

GERHARD MEIER: "Rondo," "Dann wieder die Amsel," and "Die Strasse lang pfeift eine Amsel," from *Werke,* vol. I, Zytglogge Verlag, Bern, 1987 © the Estate of Gerhard Meier.

FELICE MENGHINI: "Paesaggio grigio," from *Esplorazione,* I.E.T., Bellinzona, 1946 © Michele Menghini.

KLAUS MERZ: "Zurüsterin Nacht" and "Grosse Nacht," from *Aus dem Staub,* Haymon Verlag, Innsbruck & Vienna, 2010 © Klaus Merz.

ELISABETH MEYLAN: "Blaise Cendrars," from *Entwurf zu einer Ebene*, Verlag der Arche, Zurich, 1973 © Elisabeth Meylan.

ALBERTO NESSI: "Due poesie per la gatta," from *Rasoterra*, Casagrande, Bellinzona, 1983; "Donna in un cortile," from *Il colore della malva*, Casagrande, Bellinzona, 1992 © Alberto Nessi.

GIORGIO ORELLI:. "Sera a Bedretto," "L'ora esatta," "Nel cerchio familiare," and "Lettera da Bellinzona," from *L'ora del tempo*, Mondadori, Milan, 1962; "A Giovanna, sulle capre" and "Sinopie," from *Sinopie*, Mondadori, Milan, 1977; "Certo d'un merlo il nero . . . ," from *Spiracoli*, Mondadori, Milan, 1989; "Le forsizie del Bruderholz," "In memoria," and "Da molti anni," from *Il collo dell'anitra*, Garzanti, Milan 2001 © Giorgio Orelli

GIOVANNI ORELLI: "Det dumegna" and "G'ascia," from *Sant'Antoni dai padü*, All'insegna del pesce d'oro, Milan, 1986 © Giovanni Orelli.

ANDRI PEER: "Uclan," "Teja bandunada," "Dumengia in champogna," "Taglialaina," and "Furnatsch," from *Poesias (1946–1985)*, Desertina, Chur, 2003 © the Estate of Andri Peer.

ANNE PERRIER: "Airs grecs *(extraits)*," from *Le Joueur de flûte*, Éditions Empreintes, Lausanne, 1994 © Éditions Empreintes.

RUT PLOUDA: "Nots," "Davant il spejel," and "I naivenaivenaiva . . . ," from *Litteratura 22*, Uniun da scripturas e scripturs rumantschs, Chur, 1998 © Rut Plouda.

FABIO PUSTERLA: "Le parentesi" and "Il dronte," from *Concessione all'inverno*, Casagrande, Bellinzona, 1985; "Se potessi scegliere . . . ," and "E poi qualcuno va . . . ," from *Bocksten*, Marcos y Marcos, Milan, 1989; "Roggia" from *Pietra sangue*, Marcos y Marcos, Milan, 1999; "Lamento degli animali condotti al macello," from *Corpo stellare*, Marcos y Marcos, Milan 2010 © Fabio Pusterla.

ANTONIO ROSSI: "Spalatori di neve," from *Ricognizioni!*, Casagrande, Bellinzona, 1979 © 2001 Casagrande.

SWISS LITERATURE SERIES

In 2008, Pro Helvetia, the Swiss Arts Council, began working with Dalkey Archive Press to identify some of the greatest and most innovative authors in twentieth and twenty-first century Swiss letters, in the tradition of such world renowned writers as Max Frisch, Robert Walser, and Robert Pinget. Dalkey Archive editors met with critics and scholars in Zurich, Geneva, Basel, and Bern, and went on to prepare reports on numerous important Swiss authors whose work was deemed underrepresented in English. Developing from this ongoing collaboration, the Swiss Literature Series, launched in 2011 with Gerhard Meier's *Isle of the Dead* and Aglaja Veteranyi's *Why the Child Is Cooking in the Polenta*, has been working to remedy this dearth of Swiss writing in the Anglophone world with a bold initiative to publish four titles a year, each supplemented with marketing efforts far exceeding what publishers can normally provide for works in translation.

With writing originating from German, French, Italian, and Rhaeto-Romanic, the Swiss Literature Series will stand as a testimony to Switzerland's contribution to world literature.

SELECTED DALKEY ARCHIVE TITLES

PETROS ABATZOGLOU, *What Does Mrs. Freeman Want?*
MICHAL AJVAZ, *The Golden Age.*
The Other City.
PIERRE ALBERT-BIROT, *Grabinoulor.*
YUZ ALESHKOVSKY, *Kangaroo.*
FELIPE ALFAU, *Chromos.*
Locos.
JOÃO ALMINO, *The Book of Emotions.*
IVAN ÂNGELO, *The Celebration.*
The Tower of Glass.
DAVID ANTIN, *Talking.*
ANTÓNIO LOBO ANTUNES, *Knowledge of Hell.*
The Splendor of Portugal.
ALAIN ARIAS-MISSON, *Theatre of Incest.*
IFTIKHAR ARIF AND WAQAS KHWAJA, EDS.,
Modern Poetry of Pakistan.
JOHN ASHBERY AND JAMES SCHUYLER,
A Nest of Ninnies.
ROBERT ASHLEY, *Perfect Lives.*
GABRIELA AVIGUR-ROTEM, *Heatwave and Crazy Birds.*
HEIMRAD BÄCKER, *transcript.*
DJUNA BARNES, *Ladies Almanack.*
Ryder.
JOHN BARTH, *LETTERS.*
Sabbatical.
DONALD BARTHELME, *The King.*
Paradise.
KÜRŞAT BAŞAR, *Music by My Bedside.*
SVETISLAV BASARA, *Chinese Letter.*
MIQUEL BAUÇÀ, *The Siege in the Room.*
RENÉ BELLETTO, *Dying.*
MAREK BIEŃCZYK, *Transparency.*
MARK BINELLI, *Sacco and Vanzetti Must Die!*
ANDREI BITOV, *Pushkin House.*
ANDREJ BLATNIK, *You Do Understand.*
LOUIS PAUL BOON, *Chapel Road.*
My Little War.
Summer in Termuren.
ROGER BOYLAN, *Killoyle.*
IGNÁCIO DE LOYOLA BRANDÃO,
Anonymous Celebrity.
The Good-Bye Angel.
Teeth under the Sun.
Zero.
BONNIE BREMSER, *Troia: Mexican Memoirs.*
CHRISTINE BROOKE-ROSE, *Amalgamemnon.*
BRIGID BROPHY, *In Transit.*
MEREDITH BROSNAN, *Mr. Dynamite.*
GERALD L. BRUNS, *Modern Poetry and the Idea of Language.*
EVGENY BUNIMOVICH AND J. KATES, EDS.,
Contemporary Russian Poetry: An Anthology.
DROR BURSTEIN, *Kin.*
GABRIELLE BURTON, *Heartbreak Hotel.*
MICHEL BUTOR, *Degrees.*
Mobile.
Portrait of the Artist as a Young Ape.
G. CABRERA INFANTE, *Infante's Inferno.*
Three Trapped Tigers.
JULIETA CAMPOS,
The Fear of Losing Eurydice.
ANNE CARSON, *Eros the Bittersweet.*
ORLY CASTEL-BLOOM, *Dolly City.*
CAMILO JOSÉ CELA, *Christ versus Arizona.*
The Family of Pascual Duarte.
The Hive.
LOUIS-FERDINAND CÉLINE, *Castle to Castle.*

Conversations with Professor Y.
London Bridge.
Normance.
North.
Rigadoon.
MARIE CHAIX, *The Laurels of Lake Constance.*
Silences, or a Woman's Life.
HUGO CHARTERIS, *The Tide Is Right.*
JEROME CHARYN, *The Tar Baby.*
ERIC CHEVILLARD, *Demolishing Nisard.*
LUIS CHITARRONI, *The No Variations.*
MARC CHOLODENKO, *Mordechai Schamz.*
JOSHUA COHEN, *Witz.*
EMILY HOLMES COLEMAN, *The Shutter of Snow.*
BERNARD COMMENT, *The Shadow of Memory.*
ROBERT COOVER, *A Night at the Movies.*
STANLEY CRAWFORD, *Log of the S.S. The Mrs Unguentine.*
Some Instructions to My Wife.
ROBERT CREELEY, *Collected Prose.*
RENÉ CREVEL, *Putting My Foot in It.*
RALPH CUSACK, *Cadenza.*
SUSAN DAITCH, *L.C.*
Storytown.
NICHOLAS DELBANCO, *The Count of Concord.*
Sherbrookes.
NIGEL DENNIS, *Cards of Identity.*
PETER DIMOCK, *George Anderson.*
A Short Rhetoric for Leaving the Family.
ARIEL DORFMAN, *Konfidenz.*
COLEMAN DOWELL,
The Houses of Children.
Island People.
Too Much Flesh and Jabez.
ARKADII DRAGOMOSHCHENKO, *Dust.*
RIKKI DUCORNET, *The Complete Butcher's Tales.*
The Fountains of Neptune.
The Jade Cabinet.
The One Marvelous Thing.
Phosphor in Dreamland.
The Stain.
The Word "Desire."
WILLIAM EASTLAKE, *The Bamboo Bed.*
Castle Keep.
Lyric of the Circle Heart.
JEAN ECHENOZ, *Chopin's Move.*
STANLEY ELKIN, *A Bad Man.*
Boswell: A Modern Comedy.
Criers and Kibitzers, Kibitzers and Criers.
The Dick Gibson Show.
The Franchiser.
George Mills.
The Living End.
The MacGuffin.
The Magic Kingdom.
Mrs. Ted Bliss.
The Rabbi of Lud.
Van Gogh's Room at Arles.
FRANÇOIS EMMANUEL, *Invitation to a Voyage.*
ANNIE ERNAUX, *Cleaned Out.*
SALVADOR ESPRIU, *Ariadne in the Grotesque Labyrinth.*
LAUREN FAIRBANKS, *Muzzle Thyself.*
Sister Carrie.
LESLIE A. FIEDLER, *Love and Death in the American Novel.*

SELECTED DALKEY ARCHIVE TITLES

JUAN FILLOY, *Faction.*
Op Oloop.
ANDY FITCH, *Pop Poetics.*
GUSTAVE FLAUBERT, *Bouvard and Pécuchet.*
KASS FLEISHER, *Talking out of School.*
FORD MADOX FORD,
The March of Literature.
JON FOSSE, *Aliss at the Fire.*
Melancholy.
MAX FRISCH, *I'm Not Stiller.*
Man in the Holocene.
CARLOS FUENTES, *Adam in Eden.*
Christopher Unborn.
Distant Relations.
Terra Nostra.
Vlad.
Where the Air Is Clear.
TAKEHIKO FUKUNAGA, *Flowers of Grass.*
WILLIAM GADDIS, *J R.*
The Recognitions.
JANICE GALLOWAY, *Foreign Parts.*
The Trick Is to Keep Breathing.
WILLIAM H. GASS, *Cartesian Sonata*
and Other Novellas.
Finding a Form.
A Temple of Texts.
The Tunnel.
Willie Masters' Lonesome Wife.
GÉRARD GAVARRY, *Hoppla! 1 2 3.*
Making a Novel.
ETIENNE GILSON,
The Arts of the Beautiful.
Forms and Substances in the Arts.
C. S. GISCOMBE, *Giscome Road.*
Here.
Prairie Style.
DOUGLAS GLOVER, *Bad News of the Heart.*
The Enamoured Knight.
WITOLD GOMBROWICZ,
A Kind of Testament.
PAULO EMÍLIO SALES GOMES, *P's Three*
Women.
KAREN ELIZABETH GORDON, *The Red Shoes.*
GEORGI GOSPODINOV, *Natural Novel.*
JUAN GOYTISOLO, *Count Julian.*
Exiled from Almost Everywhere.
Juan the Landless.
Makbara.
Marks of Identity.
PATRICK GRAINVILLE, *The Cave of Heaven.*
HENRY GREEN, *Back.*
Blindness.
Concluding.
Doting.
Nothing.
JACK GREEN, *Fire the Bastards!*
JIŘÍ GRUŠA, *The Questionnaire.*
GABRIEL GUDDING,
Rhode Island Notebook.
MELA HARTWIG, *Am I a Redundant*
Human Being?
JOHN HAWKES, *The Passion Artist.*
Whistlejacket.
ELIZABETH HEIGHWAY, ED., *Contemporary*
Georgian Fiction.
ALEKSANDAR HEMON, ED.,
Best European Fiction.
AIDAN HIGGINS, *Balcony of Europe.*
A Bestiary.
Blind Man's Bluff
Bornholm Night-Ferry.

Darkling Plain: Texts for the Air.
Flotsam and Jetsam.
Langrishe, Go Down.
Scenes from a Receding Past.
Windy Arbours.
KEIZO HINO, *Isle of Dreams.*
KAZUSHI HOSAKA, *Plainsong.*
ALDOUS HUXLEY, *Antic Hay.*
Crome Yellow.
Point Counter Point.
Those Barren Leaves.
Time Must Have a Stop.
NAOYUKI II, *The Shadow of a Blue Cat.*
MIKHAIL IOSSEL AND JEFF PARKER, EDS.,
Amerika: Russian Writers View the
United States.
DRAGO JANČAR, *The Galley Slave.*
GERT JONKE, *Awakening to the Great Sleep*
War.
The Distant Sound.
Geometric Regional Novel.
Homage to Czerny.
The System of Vienna.
JACQUES JOUET, *My Beatuiful Bus.*
Mountain R.
Savage.
Upstaged.
CHARLES JULIET, *Conversations with*
Samuel Beckett and Bram van
Velde.
MIEKO KANAI, *The Word Book.*
YORAM KANIUK, *Life on Sandpaper.*
LUZIUS KELLER, ED., *Modern and*
Contemporary Swiss Poetry: An
Anthology.
HUGH KENNER, *The Counterfeiters.*
Flaubert, Joyce and Beckett:
The Stoic Comedians.
Joyce's Voices.
DANILO KIŠ, *The Attic.*
Garden, Ashes.
The Lute and the Scars
Psalm 44.
A Tomb for Boris Davidovich.
ANITA KONKKA, *A Fool's Paradise.*
GEORGE KONRÁD, *The City Builder.*
TADEUSZ KONWICKI, *A Minor Apocalypse.*
The Polish Complex.
MENIS KOUMANDAREAS, *Koula.*
ELAINE KRAF, *The Princess of 72nd Street.*
JIM KRUSOE, *Iceland.*
AYŞE KULIN, *Farewell: A Mansion in*
Occupied Istanbul.
EWA KURYLUK, *Century 21.*
EMILIO LASCANO TEGUI, *On Elegance*
While Sleeping.
ERIC LAURRENT, *Do Not Touch.*
HERVÉ LE TELLIER, *The Sextine Chapel.*
A Thousand Pearls (for a Thousand
Pennies)
VIOLETTE LEDUC, *La Bâtarde.*
EDOUARD LEVÉ, *Autoportrait.*
Suicide.
MARIO LEVI, *Istanbul Was a Fairy Tale.*
SUZANNE JILL LEVINE, *The Subversive*
Scribe: Translating Latin
American Fiction.
DEBORAH LEVY, *Billy and Girl.*
Pillow Talk in Europe and Other
Places.
JOSÉ LEZAMA LIMA, *Paradiso.*

SELECTED DALKEY ARCHIVE TITLES

JULIÁN RÍOS, *The House of Ulysses.*
  Larva: A Midsummer Night's Babel.
  Poundemonium.
  Procession of Shadows.
AUGUSTO ROA BASTOS, *I the Supreme.*
ALAIN ROBBE-GRILLET, *Project for a*
  Revolution in New York.
DANIËL ROBBERECHTS, *Arriving in Avignon.*
JEAN ROLIN, *The Explosion of the*
  Radiator Hose.
OLIVIER ROLIN, *Hotel Crystal.*
ALIX CLEO ROUBAUD, *Alix's Journal.*
JACQUES ROUBAUD, *The Form of a*
  City Changes Faster, Alas, Than
  the Human Heart.
  The Great Fire of London.
  Hortense in Exile.
  Hortense Is Abducted.
  The Loop.
  Mathematics:
  The Plurality of Worlds of Lewis.

  The Princess Hoppy.
  Some Thing Black.
LEON S. ROUDIEZ, *French Fiction Revisited.*
RAYMOND ROUSSEL, *Impressions of Africa.*
VEDRANA RUDAN, *Night.*
STIG SÆTERBAKKEN, *Self-Control.*
  Siamese.
LYDIE SALVAYRE, *The Company of Ghosts.*
  Everyday Life.
  The Lecture.
  Portrait of the Writer as a
  Domesticated Animal.
  The Power of Flies.
LUIS RAFAEL SÁNCHEZ,
  Macho Camacho's Beat.
SEVERO SARDUY, *Cobra & Maitreya.*
NATHALIE SARRAUTE,
  Do You Hear Them?
  Martereau.
  The Planetarium.
ARNO SCHMIDT, *Collected Novellas.*
  Collected Stories.
  Nobodaddy's Children.
  Two Novels.
ASAF SCHURR, *Motti.*
CHRISTINE SCHUTT, *Nightwork.*
GAIL SCOTT, *My Paris.*
DAMION SEARLS, *What We Were Doing*
  and Where We Were Going.
JUNE AKERS SEESE,
  Is This What Other Women Feel Too?
  What Waiting Really Means.
BERNARD SHARE, *Inish.*
  Transit.
AURELIE SHEEHAN, *Jack Kerouac Is Pregnant.*
VIKTOR SHKLOVSKY, *Bowstring.*
  A Hunt for Optimism.
  Knight's Move.
  A Sentimental Journey:
  Memoirs 1917–1922.
  Energy of Delusion: A Book on Plot.
  Literature and Cinematography.
  Theory of Prose.
  Third Factory.
  Zoo, or Letters Not about Love.
CLAUDE SIMON, *The Invitation.*
PIERRE SINIAC, *The Collaborators.*
KJERSTI A. SKOMSVOLD, *The Faster I Walk,*
  the Smaller I Am.

JOSEF ŠKVORECKÝ, *The Engineer of*
  Human Souls.
GILBERT SORRENTINO,
  Aberration of Starlight.
  Blue Pastoral.
  Crystal Vision.
  Imaginative Qualities of Actual
  Things.
  Mulligan Stew.
  Pack of Lies.
  Red the Fiend.
  The Sky Changes.
  Something Said.
  Splendide-Hôtel.
  Steelwork.
  Under the Shadow.
W. M. SPACKMAN, *The Complete Fiction.*
ANDRZEJ STASIUK, *Dukla.*
  Fado.
GERTRUDE STEIN, *Lucy Church Amiably.*
  The Making of Americans.
  A Novel of Thank You.
LARS SVENDSEN, *A Philosophy of Evil.*
PIOTR SZEWC, *Annihilation.*
GONÇALO M. TAVARES, *Jerusalem.*

  Joseph Walser's Machine.
  Learning to Pray in the Age of
  Technique.
LUCIAN DAN TEODOROVICI,
  Our Circus Presents . . .
NIKANOR TERATOLOGEN, *Assisted Living.*
STEFAN THEMERSON, *Hobson's Island.*
  The Mystery of the Sardine.
  Tom Harris.
TAEKO TOMIOKA, *Building Waves.*
JOHN TOOMEY, *Huddleston Road.*
  Sleepwalker.
JEAN-PHILIPPE TOUSSAINT, *The Bathroom.*
  Camera.
  Monsieur.
  Reticence.
  Running Away.
  Self-Portrait Abroad.
  Television.
  The Truth about Marie.
DUMITRU TSEPENEAG, *Hotel Europa.*
  The Necessary Marriage.
  Pigeon Post.
  Vain Art of the Fugue.
ESTHER TUSQUETS, *Stranded.*
DUBRAVKA UGRESIC, *Lend Me Your Character.*
  Thank You for Not Reading.
TOR ULVEN, *Replacement.*
MATI UNT, *Brecht at Night.*
  Diary of a Blood Donor.
  Things in the Night.
ÁLVARO URIBE AND OLIVIA SEARS, EDS.,
  Best of Contemporary Mexican Fiction.
ELOY URROZ, *Friction.*
  The Obstacles.
LUISA VALENZUELA, *Dark Desires and*
  the Others.
  He Who Searches.
MARJA-LIISA VARTIO, *The Parson's Widow.*
PAUL VERHAEGHEN, *Omega Minor.*
AGLAJA VETERANYI, *Why the Child Is*
  Cooking in the Polenta.
BORIS VIAN, *Heartsnatcher.*
LLORENÇ VILLALONGA, *The Dolls' Room.*
TOOMAS VINT, *An Unending Landscape.*

SELECTED DALKEY ARCHIVE TITLES

SERENA VITALE, *Shklovsky: Witness to an Era.*
ORNELA VORPSI, *The Country Where No One Ever Dies.*
AUSTRYN WAINHOUSE, *Hedyphagetica.*
PAUL WEST, *Words for a Deaf Daughter & Gala.*
CURTIS WHITE, *America's Magic Mountain.*
   The Idea of Home.
   Memories of My Father Watching TV.
   Monstrous Possibility: An Invitation to Literary Politics.
   Requiem.
DIANE WILLIAMS, *Excitability: Selected Stories.*
   Romancer Erector.
DOUGLAS WOOLF, *Wall to Wall.*
   Ya! & John-Juan.
JAY WRIGHT, *Polynomials and Pollen.*
   The Presentable Art of Reading Absence.
PHILIP WYLIE, *Generation of Vipers.*
MARGUERITE YOUNG, *Angel in the Forest.*
   Miss MacIntosh, My Darling.
REYOUNG, *Unbabbling.*
VLADO ŽABOT, *The Succubus.*
ZORAN ŽIVKOVIĆ, *Hidden Camera.*
LOUIS ZUKOFSKY, *Collected Fiction.*
VITOMIL ZUPAN, *Minuet for Guitar.*
SCOTT ZWIREN, *God Head.*

FOR A FULL LIST OF PUBLICATIONS, VISIT:
www.dalkeyarchive.com